CONCILIUM

Religion in the Seventies

CONCILIUM

Concilium 124 (4/1979): Practical Theology

THE CHURCH AND THE RIGHTS OF MAN

Edited by

Alois Müller
and
Norbert Greinacher

THE SEABURY PRESS / NEW YORK

1979
The Seabury Press, 815 Second Avenue, New York, N.Y. 10017
ISBN: 0-8164-2232-X (pbk.) 0-8164-0430-5

T. & T. Clark Ltd., 36 George Street, Edinburgh EH2 2LQ
ISBN: 0-567-30004-8 (pbk.)

Library of Congress Catalog Card Number: 79-65695
Printed in the United States of America

CONTENTS

Part III
The Praxis

Editorial

THE FACT that practical theology takes the subject 'The Church and Human Rights' as a matter for discussion strongly suggests that human rights represent a topical task of the Church, or a challenge to her. This view is confirmed by the fact that human rights are emerging today as an important focus of all aspirations for justice and the humanisation of mankind's condition and relationships, whether personal or public. Admittedly a number of specific claims made in the name of human rights may be made for essentially propaganda purposes. Yet in contrast there stands the unbroken line of Human Rights Declarations and Conventions from the eighteenth century to the present day. We admit equally that the concept is used in political thought and action quite vaguely at times, and, particularly when the perspective of history is recalled, in ways that invite controversy. None of this exonerates us from the duty of considering the concept as it really is and has been, both in its historical roots and in the later extensions and over-tones, with the express purpose of doing justice to its historical role under modern conditions.

Against this background of our theme, we can view the universal relevance of human rights as nothing less than a God-given opportunity, a 'kairos' for the Church. Efforts have lately been made to describe more precisely the mission of the Church, and various words have been used to interpret the concept of redemption: words like peace (but defined in terms of Development), liberation, and solidarity. These concepts are sound in their explicit commitment. The Church's mission into the world can certainly signify, in endlessly diverse situations, peace, development and liberation. But it is the very sharpness of definition of these terms that is their limitation too. This can be readily seen in the difficulties of understanding which arise within the Church itself whenever the various church-regions wish to communicate clearly about themselves to one another. Urgent Church mission can certainly be described as liberation. This is particularly obvious today for Latin America. But we must also reckon with the fact that in other parts of the planet, the mission of the Church cannot be subsumed so simply under this heading: except at the cost of extending the concept arbitrarily and interpreting it afresh!

It is just at this point that the idea of human rights provides a common denominator. This concept does really lie at the root of all specific tasks. What is seen and heard as 'Demand for Rights for Human Beings as

Human Beings' turns out to be a tangible form (although not the only one) of Church service and redemptive mission. Semantically speaking, the concept of human rights has a built-in intent that is not inherent to the same extent in the other terms. The word freedom can refer to the kind of free enterprise that refuses to be baulked of its pursuit of profit anywhere in the world. The term peace can be taken to mean—and not only in the West!—the unassailable maintenance of existing power-structures. In fact the comparative arbitrariness in the content of these ideas and others like them has the effect of rousing distrust in the minds of the opposition of the day or even of 'lookers on' rather than of creating understanding. On the other hand human rights call for an evaluation of their contents. What are they? It is granted that there are some freedoms that are human rights and some that are not; likewise there is a form of peace that is a human right and other forms that are not. Considerable light could be shed on all human aspirations, both individual and communal, if they all accepted the term 'human rights' in this sense as their yardstick. Indeed it could be a service that practical theology might render both to the Church and the wider community if it presented a reference-point on the chart of human rights as the place for the Church's task.

Moral philosophers and historical and practical theologians have combined to provide this guidance in the present issue of the journal. The pattern is three-fold. Part I considers the concept in the light of philosophical and historical studies, and in the light of biblical insights and of Church history. It immediately becomes clear that the content of the concept of human rights, as it has been handed down historically, must be enlarged. (Otherwise in border-line cases the concept would turn in on itself and become its opposite.) This enlargement can take place, for the concept has an inherent momentum towards and on evolution (W. Huber). In this regard, it is striking to observe how the most heterogeneous forces may share in the evolution of the concept from Karl Marx to Christian theology in ecumenical endeavour (J. M. Lochman). The Churches have been without the concept for a long time, but now, both consciously and instinctively the Churches and Christian thought have been impelled in the direction of human rights by the Bible. God's creative act of right should be received by his people like the impulse of an electric current—a charge of power for the powerless, the person whose human rights are constantly jeopardised by the (self-empowered) powerful. Thus the saying 'Human rights are the rights of the poor' is all too frequently proved to be an historically apt and realistic maxim (J. Limburg). The message of the New Testament goes to the root of this situation. Everyman is without power for he is a sinner; there is no such thing as a man-made righteousness. But in so far as God in Jesus Christ 'makes the sinner right (just)' he transforms the universal impossibility of mutual neighbourly love and justice into an all-pervading possibility (J. Blank). The Church has not been successful in recognising the possibility of this transformation amid the ups and downs of (sinful) human history when the historic moments of crisis have come. The Church's divided and ambiguous response to the movements towards human rights over the last two hundred years (B. Plongeron), will have to be understood now as a call to repentance (*metanoia*) and to an awareness (*ennoia*) of our truest identity.

Part II is devoted to a discussion within the churches concerning human rights. This concept, coming as it did from 'outside' is given a location in the frame of theology and ethics. There is also a search, unfortunately not altogether successful, for the reality of human rights in the life of the Church herself. This partial failure is admitted by all three articles of this section: the writers are all deeply shocked by their discovery. This is why we have consciously allowed the re-iterations to stand. When Christian faith uses the words 'human rights', all it can do is to turn back to the perspective of the Christian view of man (Christian anthropology). And that means turning back to the perspective of asking, 'Who is Christ?' (Christology) (Ch. Wackenheim). God has located man's right in Christ, in the exaltation of Jesus of Nazareth, obedient and tortured to death. The creation of human rights, as seen from the standpoint of the believing Christian means following in the footsteps of the God who is man's redeemer, and begins with God's most creative act of right in Christ.

Once this is grasped, it is clear that there is no inherent incompatibility between a 'natural' commitment to human rights and a 'supernatural' commitment to redemption, so little, one can now see, is man's transcendent fulfilment through God exhausted by his temporal elevation. It should be gratefully acknowledged that Christian intellectual effort concerning human rights has been taking place ecumenically and is bearing the fruits of ecumenism (St. Pfürtner, J. M. Lochman). This intellectual endeavour is not evading the duty and the risk of giving tangible and substantial content to a Christian ethic of human rights. It is worth noting that whereas society's most pressing problem today lies in complementing individual rights of liberty with social rights, the main issue within the Church herself is urgent championing of individual rights of liberty in regard to the power of the courts (J. A. Coriden). This is connected of course with the difference of the Church's functions when compared with the wider community.

Part III seeks to demonstrate modes of action: those that have already been taken, and those that should have been explored. The facts speak for themselves; we see for instance the difference between the approach of the over-all Church structure (R. Refoulé/L. Niilus), and the varying vistas of the wider and/or local churches. It is evident that the chief pressure-point, both of efficacy and of sacrifices, lies in the local church. (M. Goretti/S. Galilea). However, the education in awareness through centralised Church statements is not to be underrated at all, particularly in a doctrinally-oriented Church. Lastly comes the consideration of a specific problem, connected with a particular place (apartheid). This leads to the recognition that the solution of any single problem must lie in an extremely wide-ranging process, namely in new social models of behaviour (D. Hurley). The same thought lies behind consideration of the question as to what is the task of the churches of the First World: a conscientisation for politico-economic changes and basic cuts in consumption (N. Greinacher).

SUMMARY

If the Church stands for human rights she will find in the community an opportunity (kairos) for her advocacy, but she must be fully aware of a special proviso—that in these efforts more than in any other of her activities she must work extremely closely with people and institutions, and on a basis of equality. She must in no way assert herself in a role of leadership.

The Church's contribution must be genuinely her own. *She must produce concrete proposals from the heart of the Gospel.* In doing so she must never make it a condition of work with her partners that they believe in the Gospel. The work itself is dictated by the situations that arise each day, and can vary with the region. The bearers of the heaviest responsibilities therefore will be the churches at the regional and local level. The Church will need courage to venture forth; and that must be matched by courage to face failure and by willingness to learn. It is the encouragement of 'the brethren in the world' (1 Pet 5:9) that must be the main object of those words and deeds that can derive from the central leadership of the Church: *Et tu aliquando conversus confirma fratres tuos*! ('And you, when you have turned again, strengthen your brethren!') (Luke 22:32).

ALOIS MÜLLER
NORBERT GREINACHER

PART I

The Concept

Wolfgang Huber

Human Rights—A Concept and Its History

1. THE STATE OF THE PROBLEM

THE ENTRY of the concept of human rights into international law is a remarkable feature of our generation. Moreover, international law is in the process of developing beyond a law of nations to a law of mankind, and this step cannot be revoked. After several preliminary attempts by the League of Nations, the step was taken with the United Nations' Charter in 1945 and, principally, with the Universal Declaration of Human Rights on 10th December 1948.[1] Of the forty-eight states then represented at the United Nations, forty supported the Declaration; the eastern European states, South Africa and Saudi Arabia abstained from voting.

Following the Universal Declaration of Human Rights there took place the most ambitious attempt at systematisation ever undertaken by the United Nations. This was inevitable, for the transition had to be made from a general declaration to legally binding treaties at an international level which would achieve the status of law by ratification in individual states and which would be subject to an international procedure for supervision. These efforts led to the two Human Rights Treaties (or Human Rights Conventions) of 1966—and the political and legal implications of these are frequently underestimated, even today. Many would go so far as to see in the two conventions, together with the United Nations Charter, the 'kernel of a future constitution for the world'.[2]

Even though it took more than fifteen years for the transition from the Universal Declaration of Human Rights to the Human Rights Treaties to be completed, yet another decade was necessary before the required number of ratifications was at hand for the two treaties to come into effect. This happened, at first unnoticed by the public, in 1976. By January 1978 the treaties had been ratified by forty-four out of forty-six states. One of the countries which has not yet ratified them is the USA. President Carter signed the two treaties on 5th October 1977 and announced the introduction of the ratification procedure 'at the earliest possible moment'. The chances that the required proportion of American Senators—three-quarters—will agree to the ratification are regarded by many observers as slim.

It is interesting that the country in which the concept of human rights has, for the first time in the modern era, achieved an effective form and which appeals to it with particular emphasis should be one in which the attempt to give human rights a firm basis in international law has yet to be completed. This is a particularly clear example of the ambivalence which marks the concept of human rights at the present time, and this ambivalence may, in general, be expressed thus: The concept of human rights has been developed in the modern age as an *instrument of criticism*: every instance of the exercise of political and social power is subject to critical appraisal from the standpoint of human rights. However, the concept is also generally used as an *instrument of legitimation*: existing regimes receive their justification on the grounds of human rights, so that there must be as little as possible a difference between given social conditions and the demands of human rights. The attempt is therefore made, especially within the opposing social systems in countries in the northern hemisphere, to make the lack of achievement in the realm of human rights appear as little as possible, and for this, different concepts of human rights are employed in the West and in the East. In the West, human rights are understood primarily as the right to individual freedom, so the most important rights are the inviolability of the person and his privacy, the protection of property, basic legal rights and freedom of conscience, opinion and assembly. In the East, human rights are understood primarily as basic social rights, with the emphasis on equal access to education and work, health care and provision for old age. This distinction between individual and social rights still determines the discussion at the international level, and, in view of this, the perspective in which human rights in the countries of Asia, Africa and Latin America are looked at remains unconsidered. In these places it is always stressed that freedom from need and freedom from fear belong together; in the perspective of the third world the contrast between individual and social rights becomes increasingly questionable.

This contrast, as has been seen, is due to the concern for *legitimation*. When human rights are regarded with reference to their original significance as an *instrument of criticism,* it is not possible to be content with this confrontation of different concepts; a unified concept of human rights must be discovered. We shall approach the question by turning to the history of human rights; our problem is: Is there anything discernible in the historical development which could make for a unified concept of human rights? Linked with this is a further question: In view of this particular history, can universal validity be accorded to a concept of human rights which was hammered out under the specific conditions prevailing in Western Europe and North America?

2. THE HUMAN RIGHTS TREATIES AND THE HISTORY OF HUMAN RIGHTS

We may refer to the way in which the process of systematisation has been carried out in international law in order to justify the contrast between individual and social human rights. The United Nations, as we saw, has not succeeded in bringing about a unified agreement in international law for the guarantee of human rights, but it divided this between two Conventions. The first of these deals with Civil and Political Rights and the second, Economic, Social and Cultural Rights, but it is possible to see the grounds for this division not in any difference of principle between the two sets of rights but simply in the fact that the United Nations established two separate guarantee procedures for them. The newly formed Commission for Human Rights is the competent authority for the International Covenant on Civil and Political Rights. This body investigates reports from member states and may, if the member states agree, receive complaints from individuals or states. The competent body for the International Covenant on Economic, Social and Cultural Rights is the Economic and Social Council of the United Nations; a reporting procedure has been set up exclusively for investigative purposes. The Covenant on Civil and Political Rights assumes that member states will automatically pass legislation to ensure the appropriate rights, but the achievement of economic, social and cultural rights, on the other hand, is seen as a gradual process; the countries which are party to the treaty pledge themselves to do everything in order 'eventually' to achieve the full realisation of these rights (Art. 2.1 of the Covenant).

Yet the differences in the methods by which human rights are both brought into effect and guaranteed provide no reason for assuming a fundamental difference in the concept of human rights itself. Rather, the concept implies that both the establishing of conditions of freedom and the guaranteeing of freedoms already secured belong together. A glance at the history of human rights will make this clear.

The first modern formulation of human rights is contained in the Virginia Bill of Rights of 1776. A large number of very varied traditions have come together here; nothing would be more perverse than to trace human rights to one single source. One of these sources is the tradition of Roman legal thought, influenced as it is by elements of Stoic philosophy.[3] Thus the Roman jurist Gaius at the beginning of his *Institutiones* distinguishes between the civil law, which differs from nation to nation, and the 'common law of all men' (*commune omnium hominum ius*), which natural reason has set among all men. The idea that reason, as lawgiver, begets the law which is valid for all, played a major role again during the period from the sixteenth to the eighteenth century. In subsequent years the older natural law arguments were replaced by those of the law of reason.

Yet this tradition was by no means the only decisive influence on the formulation of the idea of human rights. In fact, to it were added elements of a Christian enlightenment, as it flourished above all in the eighteenth century in the Anglo-Saxon countries. It derived the inestimable value of man from the concept of his creation in the image of God. The concept of human rights thus involves a new quality over and above the Stoic/Roman tradition; it is not simply that the universal law is valid for all men equally but, primarily, that that law should protect the inestimable *value of the human person,* and this conviction comes to be a distinctive feature of the concept.

Going beyond this line of tradition, Georg Jellinek suggested more than eighty years ago that the concept of human rights was derived from the idea of freedom of conscience and religion which developed in the confessional arguments of the post-Reformation period.[4] This thesis, in view of its one-sidedness, has not been established. Certainly, the rise of human rights is unthinkable apart from the previous movements for religious freedom, but the idea of freedom of conscience is by no means the only, and certainly not the major, ground for the rise of human rights. Nevertheless, one can say that freedom of conscience and of belief is, in a primary sense, the fundamental, perhaps the most radical, human right, for in no other is the question of the absolute value of the human person raised so sharply. With the demand for freedom of faith and conscience the conviction is expressed that no governmental or social power has the right to determine a human being or to dispose of his or her humanity.

The Reformation gave expression to this 'indisposability' of the human person in the doctrine of justification; it replaced traditional philosophical definitions of man with the 'definition' that man is justified by faith. That no faith could be forced upon a man and that he could not be coerced in his conscience was indeed an inevitable consequence of this insight into Christian faith—even if it was frequently violated on all sides in the post-Reformation period.[5] It fell to secular movements to carry through this consequence of Christian faith, often in the face of ecclesiastical opposition. In order to do justice to this historical development it is essential to recognise the human rights movement for what it is—a worldy, secular phenomenon. This characteristic of the movement is ignored when the attempt is made to derive it directly from theological premises. Nevertheless, it is still possible to examine this worldly phenomenon in the light of its points of convergence with basic Christian convictions and thus to discover the grounds on which Christians today may take part in the struggle for the achievement of human rights.

The human rights movement is a worldly, secular phenomenon. One of its early stages is to be found in declarations of rights in English history—beginning with the Magna Carta in 1215, in which the rights of English barons and citizens against the crown were defined. However, with the transition from the English Bill of Rights to the first American Declaration of Rights in 1776 a qualitative step has been taken; it is not that individual rights are guaranteed, but that the power of the sovereign state as a whole is curtailed. In addition, rights are not guaranteed for a particular group of people, but for everyone. At the same time, it should, of course, be added that American rhetoric went far ahead of reality, for it was a century after the Virginia Bill of Rights before slavery was abolished, and the struggle for the elimination of racial discrimination is still going on.

Human rights require a revolutionary impulse; the inalienable rights of men and women come into play in response to the claims of princes to unrestrained power over their subordinates. The consciousness of human rights arose in the context of confrontation with the principle of absolute sovereignty.[6] It comes into play in revolutionary movements; the American War of Independence and the French Revolution paved the way for it. Human rights were demanded equally for all; their formulation was not, of course, entirely free from the limitations of class consciousness, and their content bears the stamp of an attitude of bourgeois *possessive individualism*.[7] Thus the Virginia Bill of Rights names 'the enjoyment of life and liberty, the means for the obtaining and possession of property and the pursuit and achievement of happiness and security' as inalienable human rights. The central place given to the right to property is particularly striking, and this recurs in the French Declaration of the Rights of Man and of the Citizen of 1789. It describes liberty, property, security and resistance to oppression as 'natural and irrevocable human rights'.

The role played by possessive individualism in the original formulation of the catalogue of human rights is obvious, but it would be mistaken to conclude that human rights had no significance beyond the period of the rise of middle-class consciousness. Equally, it would be mistaken to conclude that only the rights of 'possessive individualism' were claimed in the original catalogues of human rights. The Virginia Bill of Rights itself proves the contrary. After the preamble there are statements on national sovereignty and the right to control of the government; the principle of the division of powers and the right to vote follow. Then come the basic legal rights. Freedom of the press, the principle of national defence and the unity of executive power along with, finally, religious freedom conclude the document. Thus the Virginia Bill of Rights combines the right to individual freedom with the right to political involvement. Moreover, the French Declaration of Rights develops more clearly the right to equality. This is more obvious when one turns from the Declaration of 1789 to the Constitution of 1793. In Article 2 of the preamble equality, liberty, security and property are named together as fundamental human rights. Under the heading of basic social rights, the right of the needy to public assistance, the right to education and the right to social security through the co-operation of all are particularly emphasised.

The establishment of freedom by society and the protection of freedoms already secured thus belong together in the concept of human rights. It was not in the original form of the concept but rather in its specific development, particularly since the nineteenth century, that individual and social rights came to be contrasted. The present situation might well provide the occasion for the re-establishment of the original unity of the concept of human rights.

3. THE SHAPE OF HUMAN RIGHTS

From this brief survey of the contents of the earliest American and French declarations of rights the following thesis may be deduced; *freedom, equality and participation together form the shape of human rights*.[8] This triad is reminiscent of the slogan of the French Revolution: liberty, equality and fraternity. It is interesting to note, however, that the third element of the slogan, fraternity, did not find its way into the human rights documents of the Revolution. Fraternity is not a claim before the law but rather an attitude, a 'virtue' in the classical sense of the term. It is not the catalogues of *basic rights* that have developed from the slogan of the French Revolution but the *basic values* of modern politics: freedom, justice and solidarity.[9] However, the French Constitution of 1793, as we saw, named equality, freedom, security and property as the basic rights. Freedom and equality thus appear in modern political terminology in two different contexts; they occur as 'basic rights' and as 'basic values', as indications of the legal status of the person in society on the one hand, and of conscious political involvement on the other. Fraternity, however, occurs only as a basic value, while security and property are clearly basic rights. However, security thus functions as a condition for participation in the life of society; and property is seen as the legally ordered sharing in society's goods as well as (within the late eighteenth-century context) the precondition for participation in political decision-making. If this is a correct description of the function of security and property, once they are introduced as concepts within the larger concept of human rights, it is possible to justify the concept of participation alongside those of freedom and equality as the third feature within the overall concept and to see in the interaction between these three features the shape of human rights.

This conclusion will bè confirmed if we turn from the early human rights documents to those declarations by which, in our own day, human rights have found their way into international law. The Universal Declaration of Human Rights of 1948 is set out as follows: It deals first with the freedom and inviolability of the person, including his basic legal rights; then follow rights of political involvement. Social rights follow; the right to social security, to work and to choice of employment, to recreation and leisure, to an adequate standard of living, to education and to free access to culture. The elements of freedom, participation and equality are thus linked in this Declaration. That these elements were split in the Treaties of 1966 into two Covenants was clearly a matter of expediency.

Individually formulated human or basic rights usually represent particular actualisations, conditioned both by the situation and by the appropriate legal tradition, of the three features within the human rights concept. Nevertheless it would be wrong to base any one of these individual rights on just one of these features. In the face of a false one-sidedness the basic integrity of the shape must be emphasised. This hermeneutical principle might be stated thus: The three features within the shape of human rights—freedom, equality and participation—must constantly be borne in mind, both in the way they limit, and in the way they overlap with, eath other; each individual human right is to be interpreted, even when one feature is more relevant than the others, with reference to all three.

This hermeneutical principle has one major practical significance. It must be brought critically to bear on those cases in which one of the features of the shape of human rights is being stressed one-sidedly, for instance, in the case of the widespread tendency, in West Germany and other western countries, to conceive human rights as the right to freedom and thereby to narrow freedom to the individual level. It is just as valid in the eastern European context, where, both in theory and in practice, human rights are interpreted one-sidedly as the right to participation in society, and where society is viewed from the point of view of an assumed identity of the individual with the society and not from the point of view of the establishment of individual freedom.

4. THE UNIVERSALITY OF HUMAN RIGHTS

We have explained the concept of human rights against the background of the particular history which it has undergone in Europe and North

America. The results may be summarised as follows: the concept of human rights refers to the legal status of all people equally; it marks out the position of the person before the law in accordance with its conviction concerning the inviolability of the human being and must, for the sake of the value of the person, be brought into play as a regulative principle over and against all elements of state and social order. The three features of freedom, equality and participation are fundamental, and these constitute the shape of the human rights concept. Each individual human right is to be interpreted in the context of this total shape.

Understood in this way, the concept of human rights shows a close proximity to the fundamentals of Christian faith. That the fundamental rights in human society are due equally to all men arises for the Christian from the concept that all men are children of God. The inviolability of the person is a valid deduction from the theological conviction that men and women are justified before God only by faith. The basic features of freedom, equality and participation are exemplified in the position of the human person within the Body of Christ. At the same time, these motifs are radicalised in Christian faith; freedom is understood radically as the freedom of one's neighbour; equality is not cold, schematic egalitarianism, but has a marked tendency in favour of the weak, the disadvantaged and the oppressed; participation become submission. On the basis of this radicalisation the possibility arises for a critical and productive contribution on the part of Christian thought to the further development of our understanding of human rights. At the same time, this radicalisation provides the reason why Christians cannot stand indifferently outside the struggle for human rights in view of the manifest violations of those rights throughout the world.[10]

But does this constitute an answer to the question of the universality of human rights? Does not our reference to the historical development show clearly that the idea of human rights, both in its origins and in its actual form, is linked to particular historical conditions which are now outmoded? Our reflections were intended as a warning against an over-simple identification of human rights with the conditions prevailing at the time of their origin and the actual form they have assumed. Certainly, human rights do not exist independently of their concrete, historical actualisation; the claim of natural law, in its classical form, to universal validity does not necessarily entail the formulation of the hypothesis of human rights. However, the present actual form of human rights consists precisely in the fact that the concept has found its way into a form of international law which is in the process of becoming a universal human law. Neither can this form be set aside by reference to the particular conditions governing the growth of the catalogues of human rights. It is more a question of seeing that it is under these conditions for the development of human rights that a hope for a higher humanity has found expression, a humanity which can live together in society. This hope cannot simply be removed by pointing to the metaphysical background of the rise of human rights or the bourgeois basis of the human rights catalogues; it must be given its proper form for today. That which is proper for today, however, is only one form, and that must take into consideration the fact that the world which formerly was divided into separate cultural and governmental spheres has now become 'one world'. For this reason, the form of human rights must become universal; the Universal Declaration of Human Rights and the Human Rights Treaties of 1966 are of such great significance because they represent important steps on the way to such an understanding of human rights. Christian thinking can contribute something to this understanding, for Christian faith is concerned with God's desire for the world's salvation. Certainly it will not be able to have anything to do with a backward-looking universality; this would be to consider the form of the original thinking as given, and to derive ontological statements from it, ascribing to them universal validity. But it is concerned with a forward-looking universality, a universality of hope. In human rights the hope for a universal community of right finds expression; for Christians this community is a parable of that universal community which they call the kingdom of God.

Translated by Martin Kitchen

Notes

1. The texts referred to in what follows are available in several editions. They are also available in English, published by the UN in 1967, under the title *Human Rights: A Compilation of International Instruments of the United Nations.*

2. See Chr. Tomuschat 'Die Bundesrepublik Deutschland und die Menschenrechtspakte der Vereinten Nationenen. Neue Perspektiven weltweiter Verwirklichung der Menschenrechte', *Vereinte Nationen* 26, 1978, pp. 1-10, at p. 2.

3. See G. Picht 'Zum geistesgeschichtlichen Hintergrund der Lehre von den Menschenrechten: Recht im Dienst des Friedens' in *Festschrift für E. Menzel* (Berlin 1975) pp. 289-305.

4. G. Jellinek 'Die Erklärung der Menschen- und Bürgerrechte' in R. Schnur (ed.) *Zur Geschichte der Erklärung der Menschenrechte* (Darmstadt 1964) pp. 1-77.

5. See most recently on this question M. Brecht 'Die Menschenrechte in der Geschichte der Kirche' in J. Baur (ed.) *Zum Thema Menschenrechte. Theologische Versuche und Entwürfe* (Stuttgart 1977) pp. 39-96.

6. See M. Kriele *Die Menschenrechte zwischen Ost und West* (Cologne 1977) p. 9 ff.

7. See C. B. Macpherson *The Political Theory of Possessive Individualism. Hobbes to Locke* (Oxford 1962).

8. This thesis is elaborated more extensively in W. Huber and H. E. Tödt *Menschenrechte—Perspektiven einer menschlichen Welt* (2nd ed. Stuttgart 1978).

9. In the Federal Republic of Germany, both the SDP and the CDU appeal to these three basic values. This concept of 'basic values' has to be separated from another, which refers to fundamental legal rights and institutions, e.g., life, marriage, statehood etc., as 'basic values'. This two-fold use of the term 'basic values' has caused great confusion in recent German discussion.

10. See on these questions chapters V and VI of the book referred to in note 8.

Jan Milič Lochman

Ideology or Theology of Human Rights? The Problematic Nature of the Concept of Human Rights Today

1. HUMAN RIGHTS IN A DIVIDED WORLD

THE ALERT observer of the ecumenical theological scene can hardly fail to notice that human rights are moving into the centre of ecumenical interest. For years the World Council of Churches has been concerning itself with the practical and theoretical problems of human rights and finding itself again and again at breaking point over the issue. The Papal Commission, *Iustitia et Pax,* has addressed itself to the same problems and published the results of its work.[1] The confessional world-bodies have been at work on the subject for years, and the Reformed Churches have reached provisional conclusions.[2] It would seem, in fact, that Church circles have recognised human rights 'as "Kairos" for the Church'. In consequence, theological literature on the subject has grown to unmanageable proportions.

Of course this striking ecumenical convergence of interest does not mean that there is any automatic agreement as to how the vital questions should be tackled, where the emphasis should be placed, how priorities should be determined, or even how, in general, human rights should be understood and safeguarded. The question of human rights presents itself to us in a divided world, and in consequence the contemporary understanding of human rights itself betrays this 'divided' character. We hear often today of the 'Three Worlds': the Western capitalist world, the Eastern socialist world, and the Third World, consisting of the developing countries. In many respects this classification is too general and over-simplified. Nevertheless, so far as human rights are concerned, it can safely be said that they are understood in different ways in each of these three worlds.

In the *Western* view of human rights, with centuries of tradition behind it, the rights of the individual, with his inalienable dignity and certain classical prerogatives, stand in the foreground: freedom of belief and conscience, the equality of citizens before the law, legal protection for the citizen against any encroachment by the state, the right to property. . . . The insistence on such rights can be easily understood on historical grounds. They grew up in the struggle for the rights of citizens over and against traditional political and ecclesiastical institutions—in the struggle, that is, which, though it is anchored deep down in the history of western society, produced its most decisive results at the time of the American and French Revolutions, when the bourgeoisie came into its own. The classical declarations on human rights bear the marks of this origin: they protect the interests of citizens as free individuals, free producers, free property-owners.

Socialist-communist concepts of human rights are opposed to this individualistic approach and its bourgeois-capitalist outworking. Not that the intention to safeguard human dignity is in any way disputed in the socialist view, but it is more concretely conceived and more practically worked out through the establishment of social relationships which make it possible for all men, especially the hitherto underprivileged, to enjoy their personal, political and cultural, as well as their economic and social rights. This is held to be possible only in a socialist society. Hence the socialist view of human rights is determined by the objectives of the socialist society. The interests of private persons are subordinated to the rights of society.

How does the question of human rights appear from the viewpoint of the *Third World*? It is not really possible at the present time to speak of a unified doctrine of human rights in the Third World. Nevertheless the priorities of these countries are becoming clearly visible. The main concerns are: the basic need for survival in face of the famines which threaten so many; the dismantling of colonialist structures; the overcoming of racial discrimination; the achievement of cultural authenticity. The rights of individuals pale into insignificance by the side of these collective needs. In any case the promulgation of such rights would be alien to the social and cultural traditions of most parts of the Third World. The primary human right in such circumstances is the right to work and eat—essential conditions for survival; the right to greater equality of opportunity between poor and rich; the right to the ending of exploitation at national and international level.

These various concepts of human rights are not, when properly understood, mutually exclusive. But it is not always easy, amid the realities of world politics, to see how they complement each other. Far from leading to harmony, they bring tension and conflict. There are frequent clashes between the different points of view in public debate and in the discussions of international bodies.

2. PURE IDEOLOGY?

The 'divided' nature of the concept of human rights, and the fact that in different places totally different needs and interests underlie the same concept, raises a fundamental question: Is the concept of any practical use? Does the notion of human rights have any common meaning or basis? Is it not rather, in its ambiguity, a typical ideological weapon—a smoke-screen to conceal vested interests? If this last question were to be answered in the affirmative, then clearly insistence on human rights would hinder rather than help us in the quest for the mutual understanding and co-operation which are so badly needed in the world today. In that case too the growing preoccupation of the Churches with this question (a preoccupation which we noted at the beginning of this article) would be a theological damp squib, a false trail.

Such sceptical questionings of the contemporary human rights debate are strongly voiced by the political and ideological representatives of the 'Second World'. This fact may be illustrated by the negative reactions of Soviet ecclesiastical officialdom to discussions on human rights in the World Church, and by the way in which the concept of human rights was placed under taboo at the conference in Belgrade that followed up the one at Helsinki. All this does not simply result from present conditions on the political scene. The critical attitude towards human rights has a deeper historical dimension in the Marxist-socialist heritage.

Even in his younger days, Karl Marx saw the ideal of human rights in bourgeois society as a misleading expression of the self-interest of the 'haves', the questionable 'right of the strong' at work within the social structure. In other words it was for him an ideological formulation of the bourgeois worship of mammon. He wrote: 'Nothing in these so-called human rights goes beyond egoistic man—that is, beyond man as part of bourgeois society, an individual turned in upon himself, upon his own private interest and his own private whims and fancies, and alienated from the wider community.' Such an abstract ideal could never meet or eliminate the real needs of men, but would rather gloss over them. 'Man has not been liberated from religion. He has simply gained religious liberty. He has not been set free from property. He has gained freedom to own property.'[3] Behind the noble ideal of human rights lay, in short, one single interest: that of the possessor.

It is clear from the way in which Marx identifies religion directly with class-conditioned egoism that he himself is arguing from a narrow ideological standpoint. Nevertheless his critical observation that egoistic man is hovering menacingly in the background whenever human rights are discussed remains critically relevant and topical. Christians must be prepared for self-criticism at this point as they consider both Church history and the present situation. Let us just reflect on this: How often the Churches have begun to engage themselves actively and resourcefully on behalf of human rights only when their own interests were involved, their own power and influence at stake! Or how hard Church people have found it to bestir themselves, say in the matter of religious liberty, when it has not been the freedom of their own confession but that of others which has been at issue! It will do us all good therefore to reflect on Marx's criticism and apply it to ourselves—for the sake of our credibility and so of the effectiveness of our present-day concern for human rights.

We can also learn something from Marx to help us give a positive answer to the question whether a human rights programme has to do with anything more than an ideology. He forces us to check that any given stand for human rights is not just limited to one's own interests but takes into account the rights of one's fellow-men and commits itself to them—that it 'goes beyond egoistic man'. This 'going beyond'—understood in a Christian way, in terms of concrete obligation, as Jesus Christ himself understood it—becomes the criterion, and marks our passage from the ideological to the theological struggle for human rights.

3. LEARNING ECUMENICALLY

Along this line, an ecumenical 'learning process' has developed in recent years. This has produced some positive results, in spite of halting progress and occasional setbacks. Not that in this field ecumenical understanding among Christians comes easily. Ecumenical debates, like those in the world political arena, are affected and encumbered by the differing concepts and interests of the 'Three Worlds'. This state of affairs is illustrated by the passion which discussions about human rights in the World Church have constantly aroused. Their common faith does not save Christians from being caught up in the conflicts of their world. Rather it is in the very midst of these conflicts that their faith is put to the test. And yet, in spite of everything, the *common* faith survives amid all the tensions. Here lies the hope of ecumenical Christianity. The conflicts do not go away and they cannot be summarily dismissed. But they are seen in the light of a common foundation and a common goal. In this way rigid positions become more flexible. Thus there are opened up, in every human predicament, possibilities of ecumenical understanding and co-operation—possibilities which should not be underestimated even against the background of world politics.

The brief history of ecumenical discussions on human rights illustrates this possibility. There are many twists and turns in its course. It could be said that the most striking change has been the shift from the almost self-evident dominance of the western-liberal view at the beginning to the later acceptance of socialist criticism and of the Third World's concern with living standards. This process has not been a peacefully evolving one but has often shown sudden shifts of emphasis. Thus many participants from western countries were asking themselves, in the light of the debates in the World Council of Churches in the period between the General Assemblies in Uppsala and Nairobi, whether the pendulum had not swung too far in the direction of socialist and Third World concepts. In the heat of the struggle against racism in the First and Third Worlds was not too little attention being paid to the classical question of religious freedom in the Second World?

The World Council took notice of these questionings. The dialogue about human rights was intensified, and the ecumenical context helped to overcome the danger of seeing the problem in terms of false alternatives. I would mention for instance the Consultation on 'Human Rights and Christian Responsibility', which, after many years of preparation, took place in 1974 at St Pölten in Austria. There were many tensions in the Consultation, but it produced some positive results, for example in the attempt to work out a broader concept of human rights. This is shown by the following 'Analysis of Fundamental Human Rights':

(*a*) There is a fundamental right to live, involving the whole question of survival, of the threats and violations which result from unjust industrial, social and political systems, and of the quality of life.

(*b*) Men have a right to enjoy and preserve their cultural identity—a right which embraces such questions as national self-determination, the rights of minorities, and so forth.

(*c*) Men have a right to take part in decision-making within society—a right which involves the whole question of effective democracy.

(*d*) Men have a right to hold different opinions—a right which preserves a society or a system from hardening into authoritarian rigidity.

(*e*) Men have a right to personal dignity—which implies, for example, the condemnation of torture and of excessively prolonged imprisonment without trial.

(*f*) Men have a right to make a free choice of belief and religion—which implies freedom to practise that belief or religion, either alone or in fellowship with others, in public or private, through teaching, practical activity, worship and the performance of rites.[4]

The Consultation referred to this 'definition' as 'a common basis'. The description is justified to the extent that in this ecumenical catalogue of human rights a realistic concensus over the differing, yet inter-related human rights was achieved. Its consolidation, and wherever possible its development, is one of the most pressing future tasks in the ecumenical struggle over human rights. I want now to indicate more concretely two dimensions of this task (the 'horizontal' and the 'vertical').

4. COMPLEMENTARITY, COMPREHENSIVENESS, PERICHORESIS

It would be a misunderstanding of the ecumenical consensus on the complex nature of the concept of human rights if we were to conceive of it simply in terms of a pluralistic complementarity: as though each 'World', not to say each individual, having its own needs and interests, should be able to express them freely and be happy 'in its own fashion'. Such a standpoint would correspond to the ideology of 'egoistic man'. We must never confuse with it a theological theory and practice of human rights based on the normative 'word and event' of Jesus Christ. Jesus of Nazareth, as we find him in the New Testament, is, in his unreserved offering of himself to God and his fellow-men, the very antithesis of egoistic man. In contrast to the 'first' self-seeking Adam he is the 'second Adam', come 'to seek and save the lost' (Luke 19:10), out to help 'those who labour and are heavy-laden', 'the abused and deprived': the restorer of human rights in the widest, completest sense. The salvation he brings affects soul and body, the individual and society, mankind and 'groaning creation' (Romans 8:19).

The complexity of the concept of human rights in the world of today must be understood theologically in the light of what we know of Christ: not in the sense of a stabilising tension between opposing interests, but in terms of their dynamic relationship with each other. It is right and proper that in the different 'Worlds' men should fix their priorities and draw protection and strength from them at those points at which their humanity is especially threatened and oppressed. Thus in a bourgeois-capitalist world those socio-economic rights which are so often undervalued must be constantly brought to mind (participation of workers in industry, the right to work, etc.). On the other side, in a Marxist-communist society a stand must be taken for the underdeveloped rights of freedom of belief and conscience. Yet in every legitimate engagement for human rights

Christians will always be encouraged, by remembering the all-embracing salvation of Christ and the ecumenical horizon of faith, to look beyond and go beyond their own particular standpoint and to respect the rights of others with their different priorities. In any case the playing-off of one's own interests against those of others—so often practised on the political world-stage—should be ecumenically resisted. As I see it, the particular task of the Church in this field is to be outgoing towards others (using an ancient dogmatic concept, I would speak of a 'perichoresis of human rights', of their 'co-inherence'); to bear in mind the indivisibility of human rights in our divided world; and so to be 'counsel for the defence of our fellow-men's rights' (for us in the industrial countries that would mean, for example, defending the vital interests of the Third World).

This insight into the complementarity, comprehensiveness and co-inherence of human rights has its primary application in a spatial, geographical sense—keeping the ecumenical horizon open over one's own region and one's own world. But it has also a temporal dimension. It has to do with the interdependence of the generations in history. The rights of our contemporaries are not the only frame of reference for a responsible theory and practice of human rights. The way we exercise our rights affects the opportunities and rights of future generations. They must all therefore be co-ordinated. Every conscious or unconscious adoption of the *après nous le déluge* stance, whether by individuals or groups, perverts our human rights into human wrongs. This is, notoriously, the strategy of 'egoistic man'. This temporal aspect takes on a special urgency today in view of our relations with our environment. Such an understanding of human rights leads us to strive not only for economic but also for ecological justice. By its redemptive and ecumenical character, faith in Christ lays on the Christian a special responsibility in this respect too.

5. HUMAN RIGHTS BEFORE GOD

We thus come to the 'vertical' aspect of the theological understanding of human rights: to the question of the significance in this context of faith in God. Christian thinking, as well as secular thinking, sometimes shows great reserve at this point. The argument is this: Human rights concern everybody. Therefore we should avoid overstressing a definitely theological or specifically Christian view, so as not to set ourselves apart from other people. In reply we must ask: Can there be a theological understanding of man which leaves God out of account? And is it true that to emphasise the 'distinctively Christian' must necessarily involve separating oneself from one's fellow-men? For myself, I would answer both these questions in the negative, and insist on the importance of the idea of God, formulated in a Christian sense, for an ecumenical understanding of human rights. In fact it could turn out to be very helpful for an ecumenical effort on behalf of human rights, both theoretically and practically, and in the sense of a fruitful personal motivation.

Theoretically, for overcoming a too-ready acceptance of received arguments for human rights (especially perhaps the traditional liberal ones). Christian theology has in the past often called for such acceptance and has shared the limitations and prejudices associated with such 'rights', particularly their individualism and idealism, and their anthropological optimism. This tendency must today be corrected and a wider approach adopted. At this point the biblical notion of God, which concerns itself redemptively with the totality of creation and its needs, offers a liberating, open horizon. In a theological sense, human rights are in no way to be defined or constituted either as predicates of nature or some timeless 'essential humanity', or as the result of some historical-materialistic process of self-deliverance. Theologically the right to be human must be anchored in a real answerability *coram Deo* (before God).

This theoretical anchoring leads to an important *ethical* consequence, because it resists any particularistic narrowing of the concern for human rights. The formulation *coram Deo* has 'the advantage that it respects, and demands respect for, the dignity and rights of all men. By contrast any formulation based on experience must necessarily be limiting and selective, because our experience is limited and we can only conceive of what is universally human by the extrapolation of what "human" means for us.'[5] The common reference to God and his Kingdom is of the utmost importance because it gives the ecumenical commitment to human rights its openness and its sense of obligation.

Finally we must mention the inner potential of faith in God as *personal motivation* in the quest for human rights. In practice this quest is threatened from two sides: in the first place by the discouraging setbacks which so often attend entry into this field; and in the second by the rising spectre of self-righteousness which can corrupt the best intentions. Here our knowledge of the 'vertical dimension' comes to our aid, bringing both encouragement and rebuke. It saves us—to quote the document from the World Alliance of Reformed Churches—'from falling into despair when we have to put up with crushing and disheartening setbacks. . . . At the same time it prevents our exertions in the struggle for human rights leading to self-justification, to justification by works, instead of to a deep repentance and a selfless commitment to justice and freedom as the response to our own justification by the grace of God'.[6]

Understood in this way, a clearly articulated *theological* reference and the emphasis on a *Christian* perspective on human rights are not to be taken as implying an 'ecclesiastical go-it-alone', or a 'Christian solo-run' in the highly-charged field of human rights, much less as pleading for 'the preservation of Christian privileges'. On the contrary, the 'distinctively Christian', understood in the biblical sense, establishes no privileges, but drives us, as we follow Jesus, to an unconditional openness and to a commitment to others. A truly Christian understanding conceives of the rights of Christians only in the context of human rights—of *the rights of our fellow-men*.

Translated by G. W. S. Knowles

Notes

1. *Die Kirche und die Menschenrechte* (Munich and Mainz 1976).
2. *Gottes Recht und Menschenrechte* edited by J. M. Lochman and J. Moltmann (Neukirchen 1976).
3. K. Marx *Die Frühschriften* edited by S. Landshut (Stuttgart 1953) pp. 194, 198.
4. *Human Rights and Christian Responsibility* (W.C.C. Geneva 1974) p. 61.
5. J. Moltmann *Evang. Kommentare* (1976) p 282.
6. *Gottes Recht und Menschenrechte* p. 63.

James Limburg

Human Rights in the Old Testament

WHEN Jimmy Carter took the office of President of the United States, he quoted a saying from the prophet Micah as part of his inaugural address: 'He has showed you, O man, what is good; and what does the Lord require of you but to do justice, and to love kindness, and to walk humbly with your God?' (Micah 6:8)[1] This ancient call for justice is one of the best-known biblical statements on human rights. The Hebrew word translated as 'justice' in this text is *mišpāṭ*, and by investigating some of the contexts in which this noun and its cognate verb, *šāpaṭ*, appear in the Old Testament, we can discover something of the notion of human rights as expressed in that portion of Scripture.[2]

1. THE POWERLESS

We begin with a short saying from Micah's contemporary, Isaiah. He once pronounced a 'woe' (which meant he was announcing a funeral) upon the political leaders of his day: 'Woe to those who decree iniquitous decrees, and the writers who keep writing oppression, to turn aside the needy from justice [*mišpāṭ*] and to rob the poor of my people of their right, that widows may be their spoil, and that they may make the fatherless their prey!' (Isaiah 10:1-2). According to this text, failure to achieve justice involved the oppression of three groups: the poor, the widow and the orphan.

As we examine the texts where *mišpāṭ* and *šāpaṭ* occur, we discover that we keep running into this trio, sometimes with the addition of the stranger (Exodus 22:21-22) or the sojourner (Deuteronomy 24:19-22). When the Bible deals with justice, it tends to be very specific, speaking in terms of widows and orphans, poor people and strangers.

What do these groups have in common? These are the persons in any society who have no power, and who are thus easily taken advantage of. The widow has no husband to watch over her rights, the orphan has no parents, the poor has no money, and the stranger has no friends. These are the powerless, and a special concern for them runs through the entire Bible, from early OT legal text (Exodus 22:21-22) to later NT epistle (James 1:27-2:7).

2. LEGAL MATERIALS AND THE POWERLESS

When the ordinary Christian thinks of 'law' in the Bible, he thinks first of the Ten Commandments. But these commandments are probably remembered from a catechism, and in so remembering them an important clue to the proper understanding of biblical law may be neglected.

Both versions of the Decalogue in the Bible begin in the same way: 'I am the Lord your God, *who brought you out of the land of Egypt, out of the house of bondage*' (Exodus 20:2; Deuteronomy 5:6, emphasis added). The clause printed in italics, often omitted in instructional materials, is important because it furnishes a *reminder* of what God has done for his people. He has entered into a special *relationship* with them ('I am the Lord your God') and has delivered them from slavery. The commandments which follow spell out the *response* which is expected of God's people. These 'three r's' are essential for a proper understanding of law in the Bible. Biblical commandments do not define a legal relationship, in the manner of a contract. Rather, they describe the kind of response expected from a people who have already experienced God's delivering and sustaining love, and who are thus motivated to react. The various legal collections in the OT indicate the forms which that reaction ought to take.

The Book of the Covenant (Exodus 20:22-23:33) is a collection of laws coming from the period of the judges (about 1240-1020 B.C.). Here is expressed a good deal of concern for the powerless: 'You shall not wrong a stranger or oppress him, for you were strangers in the land of Egypt. You shall not afflict any widow or orphan' (Exodus 22:21-22). Note that the commandment about the stranger is motivated by a reminder of the Exodus deliverance. This is also true in Exodus 23:9. 'You shall not oppress a stranger; you know the heart of a stranger, for you were strangers in the land of Egypt.' Other laws in this collection prohibit excessive interest rates for the poor (22:25) and make provisions for them to gather from the fields every seventh year (23:10-11). The poor man should get fair treatment in the courts (23:6), but he should not be favoured just because he is poor (23:3).

The bulk of Deuteronomy consists of sermons attributed to Moses. While the book was probably composed in the seventh century B.C., like all preaching, it works from older texts and applies them to a new situation. The reminder/response pattern is evident in these sermons. Note, for example, Deuteronomy 4:37-40, which begins with a reminder of what God has done, 'And because he loved your fathers and chose their descendants after them, and brought you out of Egypt . . .' and then moves into the expected response, 'Therefore you shall keep his statutes and his commandments. . . .' This expected reaction of the people once again includes a concern for the powerless. The tithe is for their support (14:28-29; 26:12-15) and they are to be cared for with generosity (15:7-11). Employers are to pay their workers immediately and not oppress them; God watches over them (24:14-15). Legal rights of the powerless are to be guarded (14:17-18). And, in an interesting welfare distribution system, they are to be allowed to gather a portion of the harvest for themselves (24:19-22; cf. Ruth 2).

The Holiness Code in Leviticus 17-26 appears to have taken shape during the sixth century B.C., though once again it contains material which is more ancient. These commandments should be understood as describing the expected response of a people who are reminded of their special relationship to God (18:1-5; 20:26; 22:31-33). Here are directives to leave something after the harvest for the poor and sojourner (19:9-10), to give impartial judgment in the courts (19:15), to protect the stranger (19:33-34), and generally to care for the poor (25:35-38).

To summarise: Law or commandment in these collections should always be understood in the context of the covenant relationship between God and people. The people are reminded of what God has done for them, enjoy a special relationship to him, and are then expected to respond in a certain way. An important aspect of this response, as spelled out in each collection, is a particular concern for the powerless, including the widow, the orphan, the poor and the stranger.

3. PROVERBS AND THE POWERLESS

The book of Proverbs is a collection of short essays and sayings which was used in Jerusalem for the instruction of young men who would one day assume positions of leadership in Israel. While the book was produced during the time of Solomon in the tenth century (Proverbs 1:1; 10:1) and supplemented during the days of Hezekiah in the eighth century (Proverbs 25:1), its contents are more antique and reflect amazingly diverse origins. No doubt much of the material grew out of the education that took place in the family and the extended family, in the manner of folk wisdom throughout the world. But some material came from outside Israel. The section in 22:17-24:22 contains sayings borrowed from the courts of Egypt and re-shaped to fit the needs of Israel. While the texts are not certain, Proverbs 30:1 and 31:1 apparently identify materials which originated in north Arabia (cf. Genesis 25:14). Here, then, is a collection of the best of international wisdom of the time, put into a form suitable for the instruction of young future leaders in Israel.

These texts exhibit a special concern for the widow and orphan, and especially for the poor. One ought to be alert to the cry of the poor, because 'He who closes his ear to the cry of the poor will himself cry out and not be heard' (Proverbs 21:13). Those who have ought to share with the poor who do not have (22:9), and in so doing will find happiness (14:21). The righteous are expected to guard the legal rights of the poor (29:7); this is a special responsibility of the king (29:14; 31:9; cf. Psalm 72:2; 4:12-14). Among the virtues of the ideal wife is her generosity to the poor (31:20). Imperatives addressed to these young men being trained for leadership advise them to watch over the rights of the poor and orphan. If they fail to do so, God himself will take up the cause of the powerless and act as their Advocate (22:22-23; 23:10-11). It is he who keeps watch over the boundary markers at the edges of the widow's land (15:25).

Our investigation of the theme of concern for the powerless could continue by examining a number of Psalms which are prayers of the poor (Psalm 40:17; 74:19; 86:1, etc.). But the point has been made that care for the powerless is central to the expected style of life of a people of God.

4. THE PROPHETS AND THE POWERLESS

The most eloquent OT spokesmen for the powerless are the Hebrew prophets, particularly Amos, Isaiah and Micah. By focusing on texts where the words *mišpāṭ* or *šāpaṭ* appear, we can discover something of the shape of justice as expressed in their preaching.

(*a*) There is, first of all, a theological dimension to the prophetic notion of justice. Justice is the expected response of the people of God to what God has done for them. This is particularly evident in the 'Song of the Vineyard' as found in Isaiah 5:1-7. Perhaps finding himself at a vintage festival celebrating a harvest, the prophet began singing what must have seemed an innocent folk song:

> Let me sing about my friend,
> Listen while I sing you this song,
> a song of my friend and his vineyard . . . (Isa. 5:1 T.E.V.)

The friend had expended great efforts for the vineyard (5:2; note the succession of verbs) but the vineyard yielded only a crop of worthless fruit

(5:2). How could this have happened? The prophet asks his audience to act as a jury, and it was obvious that they would have to declare the 'friend' innocent and the 'vineyard' itself guilty (5:3-4). Thus the vineyard would have to be destroyed (5:5-6). But the vineyard was—the very people whom the prophet was addressing, and they had just pronounced judgment upon themselves (5:7).

Of interest for our topic is the fact that the 'fruits' which were expected of the people of Israel were justice [*mišpāṭ*] and righteousness (5:7).

(*b*) Secondly, there is a dynamic quality to this expected response. The text from Micah cited at the beginning of this article is a priest's answer to a question put by an inquiring worshipper (Micah 6:6-7). The priest says that what the Lord really wants from him is not sacrifices, but for him to 'do justice [*mišpāṭ*], and to love kindness and to walk humbly with your God'.

Two texts from Isaiah where the same vocabulary occurs point in the same direction. A series of imperatives adressed to ruler and people (Isaiah 1:10) urges them to 'do justice [the verb *šāpaṭ*] for the orphan, take up the cause of the widow' (Isaiah 1:17b, my translation). When the prophet accuses his nation's political leaders of associating with underworld characters and accepting bribes (Isaiah 1:23a), he also says, 'They do not do justice [the verb, *šāpaṭ*] for the orphan, and the widow's cause does not come before them' (Isaiah 1:23b, my translation).

A well-known text from Amos again indicates the dynamic nature of 'doing justice'. After announcing that God has rejected Israel's liturgical worship (Amos 5:21-23), the prophet tells his hearers what God really wants: 'Let justice [*mišpāṭ*] roll down like waters, and righteousness like an ever-flowing stream' (5:24). Abraham Heschel comments on this passage, 'One is uncertain of the exact meaning of this bold image. It seems to combine several ideas: a surging movement, a life-bringing substance, a dominant power. . . . Justice is not a mere norm, but a fighting challenge, a restless drive.'[3]

(*c*) How should this 'fighting movement' express itself? The prophetic texts impress upon us yet a third aspect of doing justice, which we shall name the sociological dimension. In these sermons which speak of justice, we keep running into people, specifically that familiar trio of the widow, the orphan and the poor (Isaiah 1:17, 23; 3:14-15; 10:2). These are the people not represented when unfavourable legislation is passed (10:1-2). They do not get fair treatment in the courts (Isaiah 1:23; 5:23; 10:2; cf. Amos 5:7, 10-11; 5:12). To 'do justice' means to take up their cause by acting as their advocates. Political leaders and people are exhorted to do so (Isaiah 1:16b-17; see the comments above) and are accused of having failed to act as advocates for the powerless (Isaiah 1:23, discussed above).

(*d*) What happens when a people and its leaders fail to 'do justice'? In language which recalls Proverbs 22:22-23, Isaiah announces that the case of the People v. Political Leaders has come to a higher court, with God himself acting as Advocate for the people:

> The Lord has taken His place to make an accusation,
> He stands to judge nations.
> The Lord comes with a case [*mišpāṭ*]
> against the elders and princes of His people:
> 'It's you who have devoured the vineyard,
> the spoil of the poor is in your houses.
> What do you mean by crushing My people,
> by grinding the face of the poor?'
> —says the Lord God of hosts.
> (Isaiah 3:13-15, my translation).

Such a nation will have to face the purging fires of God's judgment, but will one day emerge as a purified community (Isaiah 1:21-26)

(*e*) Finally, there is the promise that in the future God will build a new city, with justice and righteousness as the very standards for its construction (Isaiah 28:17). Then a king from the line of David will appear and his administration will be marked by lasting peace, justice and righteousness (Isaiah 9:7). This new son of Jesse, this 'new David', will be especially concerned about the powerless, '. . . with righteousness he shall judge [*šāpaṭ*] the poor, and decide with equity for the meek of the earth' (Isaiah 11:4a).

To summarise our investigation of the prophetic material: 'Doing justice' in the prophetic manner means the People of God responding to what God has done for them. Their response takes the form of assuming a role of advocacy for the powerless. When God's people fail in this role, they can expect to face his judgment. God himself acts as Advocate for the powerless, and will one day finally establish peace, justice and righteousness.

5. HUMAN RIGHTS AND DOING JUSTICE

The most common image used in connection with justice in the West is a scale, symbolising the balancing of the human rights of one side with those of another.[4] The prophetic picture associated with justice is not a scale, but a mighty, surging stream (Amos 5:24).

The comparison of these two images can give us the clue to the OT's understanding of justice. These Scriptures do not speak of 'justice' as a static, quiet state, where balance has been achieved. Rather, they summon a people to 'do justice', responding to what their God has done for them by acting as advocates for the widow and the orphan, the stranger and the poor.

Notes

1. Biblical quotations are from the Revised Standard Version, unless otherwise indicated.
2. Themes expressed in this article are developed more fully in my book *The Prophets and the Powerless* (Atlanta: John Knox Press, 1977).
3. A. Heschel *The Prophets* (New York: Harper, 1969) p. 212.
4. See the comments of Heschel *loc. cit.*

Josef Blank

The Justice of God as the Humanisation of Man—the Problem of Human Rights in the New Testament

1. THE OT HEBREW AND HELLENISTIC BACKGROUND

1.1. At first glance the NT might appear to be much less fruitful as a source for the justification of human rights than the OT. In the OT we find legal thinking which reveals a 'humanising tendency' in the multiplicity of written sources. That is to say: in the OT we see an ever increasing awareness of the special position of man and the dignity of man. We see human life and the basic necessities of life rising to the top of the scale of ethical-legal values. This is seen most clearly expressed in the 'theologumenon' of man's Creation in the 'image of God' (Gen. 1:26 f.; 5:1-3:9, 6). However one interprets this concept of 'man's reflection of the image of God',[1] one thing at any rate is clear, namely, that this idea (Gen. 9:6) should be the basis for forbidding the spilling of human blood.

> 'He who sheds man's blood,
> shall have his blood shed by man,
> for in the image of God
> man is made.' (*Jerusalem Bible*, Gen. 9:6.)

Anyone who murders a human being desecrates the image of God. Thereby in principle we have reached the idea of a 'human right', which is justified in terms of the dignity of man. Human dignity and human rights belong together. No human right without human dignity: no human dignity without human right. These axioms are implied in the biblical view of God's relations with man and man's relationship to God. P. formulates this relationship to God as being extablished with the creation of man. This insight, however, presupposes the special theological experience of Israel through its history. Accordingly it is no accident that Church and theology in the course of their history have perceived in this thought of 'the creation of man in the image of God' a significant starting-point for their view of the principle of the equality of all men.

1.2. This is also confirmed for us by the Hebrew doctrine of the 'naochitic Commandments', which apply to all men, as compared with Moses-Torah which applies only to Israel.[2] Its contents concern the commandment to observe the lawn the commandment forbidding blasphemy against God, worship of idols, vices, the spilling of blood, robbery, the consumption of the member severed from a living animal (Tractate-Sanhedrin 56a). In this too we can detect the endeaoour to discern beside the law of Israel a basic minimum of ethico-legal norms applicable to mankind as a whole. It would appear to be likely that the 'Apostles' Decree': 'You are to abstain from food sacrificed to idols, from blood, from the meat of strangled animals and from fornication' (*Jerusalem Bible*, Acts 15:20; 15:29) is a decree designed to facilitate living together in a mixed community consisting of Jewish-Christians and 'Heathen'-convert-Christians, and it took its guidance from the model of the 'naochitic Commandments'.[3] With regard to the ethical commandments, such as the Decalogue, no difficulties of principle were involved.

1.3. In the Inter-Testamental period, interesting developments are linked to the above, especially in the Hellenistic and Hellenic-Jewish sphere. What is involved here is the development and spread of the idea of humanity ('*Philanthropia*') (lat. '*humanitas*') during the Hellenistic period.[4] The demand for humanity, above all under the influence of the Stoa, becomes the 'basic attitude of mind linking all civilised humanity'.[5] Hellenistic-Judaism also allowed itself to be gripped by this idea of humanity.[6] The most impressive testimony proving this is the tractate by Philo on Alexandria, writing about '*philanthropia*'—'*humanitas*' in his work 'On the Virtues' ('*De Virtutibus*').[7]

In this tractate 'On the Virtues', Philo undertakes the task of claiming 'humanity' for Moses and the OT Law, and he merits close attention for his way of doing this. His concern is to propound an apology of Judaism, to rebut the charge made against the Jews, as it was also to be made later by Tacitus against the Christians, that they represented '*misanthropia*', embodying '*odium generis humani*', hatred of the human race.[8] In the first place, Moses the lawgiver appears as the pattern of true humanity, for the reason that when deciding the question of his successor in office Moses did not seek his own advantage nor that of his family, but on the contrary only considered what would be best for the overall good of the Jewish people. He displayed towards his people 'human kindness and loyalty'[9] and 'human kindness and a sense of community'.[10] This love towards humanity is revealed in many of the commandments of Moses, Philo asserts. Philo particularly singles out: the commandment forbidding usury, the taking of interest (Ex. 22:24; Lev. 15:36 f.; Deut. 23:20);[11] the commandment enjoining payment to poor people of the rewards of their labours immediately on the same day (Deut. 24:15; Lev. 19:13), and furthermore not for reasons of justice or fairness, but 'also because the manual worker or load carrier, who toils painfully with his whole body like a beast of burden, "lives from day to day", as the phrase goes, and his hopes rest upon his payment'.[12] Further examples of the OT Laws include the regulation that a creditor should not obtain his money from a debtor by force (Deut. 24:10 f.)[13] and the ordinance forbidding reapers or grape-pickers from making a second harvest or aftermath (Lev. 19:9 f.; Deut. 24:20-22).[14] Philo regards as special signs of OT humanity the custom of sabbath observance and the Year of Jubilee (Lev. 25).[15] Particular humanity has to be shown towards 'proselytes' or incomers: one should love the proselytes as oneself.[16] Strangers and foreign immigrant guest-workers should also be included in this philanthropical love.[17] Likewise, Philo points out 'there are other charitable and very merciful regulations as to the treatment of enemies in wartime', and OT examples are adduced in proof.[18] The same is true of laws concerning slaves.[19] According to Philo, humanity should not, however, be restricted only to strangers, enemies and slaves, but should be extended also to 'animals of irrational nature'[20] and 'plants and vegetation'.[21] With regard to the plant-world, Philo draws attention to the ordinance to spare the stock of trees during the siege of a town (Sections 149-154) (Deut. 20:19 ff.), a regulation counter to the usual widespread practice in wartimem Philo attacks strongly the heathen custom of exposing unwanted newborn children. This to Philo is the very opposite of humanity: it represents hostility against the human race.[22] It will not come as a surprise to us after all this to find Philo describing God Himself as '*philanthropos*', as loving mankind.[23] God the 'lover of men' is the true friend of man:[24] humanity means true imitation of God.[25] Pride and arrogance, on the contrary, are vices which overstep the limits of human nature leading some individual to hold himself to be, 'neither man nor demigod, but wholly divine', vices which lead to inhumanity. 'Slaves he treats as cattle, the free as slaves, kinsfolk as strangers, friends as parasites, fellow-citizens as foreigners'.[26] Philo did not have far to look for examples of such inhumane behaviour: he only had to think of his own experience with the emperor Caligula. The object of all Moses' legislation is to create 'unanimity, neighbourliness, fellowship, reciprocity of feeling, whereby houses and cities and nations and countries and the whole human race may advance to supreme happiness'. Philo adds that 'hitherto, indeed these things live only in our prayers, but they will, I am convinced, become facts beyond all dispute, if God, even as he gives us the yearly fruits, grants that the virtues should bear abundantly. And may some share in them be given to us, who from well-nigh our earliest days have carried with us the yearning to possess them'.[27]

When one considers Philo's exposition of humanity in the OT, one sees that he has a firm grasp of the essential points and has utilised them well for his purpose. Philo's ideal of humanity has attained a high ethical and social level, a level so lofty that it cannot be easily surpassed. Accordingly it is worth looking at the NT in the light of this and seeking out what is really new in the NT Christian definition of humanity. Here we must be on our guard against making false exaggerated claims, and we must also look for the definition of the ideal in its proper place. We must look for humanity in the context of the various basic trends and tendencies we have already found in Philo, and compare this with the NT contexts and perspectives.

2. NEW TESTAMENT PERSPECTIVES

2.1. Let us begin with the concept of '*philanthropia*' in context. There are three relevant passages.

2.1.1. We read in Acts 27 how Julius the centurion, who had the task of bringing the Apostle Paul before the imperial tribunal in Rome, displayed towards Paul a humane attitude, allowing Paul, when they put in at Sidon, to visit his fellow-believers (Acts 27:3). Likewise, the inhabitants of Malta, even though they were barbarians, behaved with extraordinary kindness and humanity towards Paul when he was rescued from shipwreck (Acts 28:2).

2.1.2. The most important passage is, however, undoubtedly: Titus 3:4-6. 'But when the kindness and love of God our saviour for mankind were revealed, it was not because he was concerned with any righteous actions we might have done ourselves; it was for no reason except his own compassion that he saved us, by means of the cleansing water of rebirth and by renewing us with the Holy Spirit which he has so generously poured over us through Jesus Christ our saviour. He did this so that we should be justified by his grace, to become heirs looking forward to inheriting eternal live' (*Jerusalem Bible,* Titus 3:4-7).[28] Here the concept of God's love for mankind, which as we saw occurs already in Philo, is used in order to interpret anew the Pauline doctrine of justification. God does not justify man on the basis of man's 'righteous actions' but only through his own gracious compassion. God is here acting in accordance with the ethos of humanity prevalent in late classical antiquity. A further aspect is added. Whereas Philo sees God's love towards men as becoming visible above all in the precepts of the Torah, in the case of the writer of the letter to Titus, the appearance of God's love towards mankind is bound to the person of Jesus Christ. The abstract concept of '*humanitas Dei*' when linked with the person of Jesus Christ gains concrete physical dimensions we can comprehend and is filled with meaning. Jesus Christ embodies in human form this divine 'humanitas'.

What we have here is the Hellenistic interpretation of the Pauline doctrine of justification and the Christology which accompanies it. We are led to the conclusion that, if Jesus Christ's divine act of salvation represents the highest expression of the humanity of God, then the ideal of '*humanitas*' in classical antiquity can also be interpreted fundamentally in a Christian sense. God's unconditional compassion in his dealings with mankind becomes the pattern for Christian humane behaviour. Christianity and '*humanitas*' are clearly convergent.

2.2. The passages under consideration show us how we are to approach the problem of human rights in the NT—namely, on the basis of the Gospel and accepting the Gospel premisses.

2.2.1. This applies firstly to the proclamation of the historic Jesus. If we compare the kerygma with Philo's pronouncements, with their lofty ethical level, we are immediately struck by the entirely different starting-point. Philo adopts the standards handed down by Graeco-philosophic ethics, and adapts them to OT conditions. Jesus, on the other hand, acts as an eschatological prophet: his starting point is eschatology. This is especially true of Jesus' proclamation of the proximity of the Kingdom of God. Nowadays in exegesis there is virtual consensus that the 'Kingdom of God' refers to ultimate final salvation in its full unrestricted sense. 'God is the Lord of history and grants men salvation by virtue of His almighty sovereignty; that is the tenor of the biblical message of the "Kingdom of God" which we nowadays find a difficult remote concept'.[29] This, however, implies that God enforces His lordship in the world, enforces His divine justice, by giving mankind His backing, taking sides and taking up the apparently lost cause of man into His own hands, in order to achieve the freedom and salvation of mankind. Jesus Christ is aware of his position as representative of God in his liberating saving lordship. 'But if it is through the finger of God that I cast out devils then know that the kingdom of God has overtaken you' (*Jerusalem Bible,* Luke 11:20; cf. Matt. 12:28). What is the crux here? The OT knows, especially in the Psalms, the thought that it is God himself who champions the special rights of the weak, the poor, the oppressed, and the innocent who are persecuted, the widow and the orphan. According to these testimonies God is not only 'the supreme guarantee of the rule of justice', the origin and source of all law—that is the usual view—but indeed God in the OT is seen as God who helps the person who has no aid to obtain what is his right. God does not primarily stand on the side of the mighty and powerful who have the machinery of justice at their disposal and manipulate it for their own interests, rather he is on the side of the victims of injustice. It is interesting to see that the protection under the law of those who are lacking in rights, and those who are oppressed, is one of the special tasks of the king who is the 'anointed of Yahweh':

> He will free the poor man who calls to him,
> and those who need help,
> he will have pity on the poor and feeble,
> and save the lifes of those in need; . . . (*Jerusalem Bible*, Psalm 72:12-13).[30]

The Messhiah too is to fulfil this task, according to the well-known text in Isaiah 11:1-10.[31] Likewise, according to Isaiah 61:1-3, the 'Anointed of Yahweh' is described as proclaiming 'liberty to captives, freedom to those in prison'.[32] Therefore it is assuredly no coincidence when Luke recalls precisely this text as the basis of the 'inaugural discourse' of Jesus in Nazareth (Luke 4:14-30). If, as we can assume, this text at Isaiah 61:1 f. is a significant characterisation of Jesus Christ's vision of his own role, then Jesus apparently saw himself above all as the messianic helper and liberator of the underprivileged, the oppressed and the poor. The beatitudes (Luke 6:20-23; Matt. 5:3-12) confirm this impression.[33]

2.2.2. Jesus champions the poor, those who mourn, those who are deprived of their legal rights or are illegally mistreated, who have been swindled, abased and insulted, those who exist on the fringes of Jewish society, those who are 'publicans and sinners'. Jesus is thus quite demonstratively taking sides and he celebrates with these people the Eucharist, the feast of the Kingdom of God.[34] In the circle of his own disciples Jesus treats women with complete equality, and this is bound to have been interpreted in Jewish society of the time as a symbolic provocation and challenge. In her impressive book *Jesus der Mann*,[35] Hanna Wolff brings out the surprisingly novel attitude which Jesus demonstrates with regard to women. Whereas in contemporary Judaism many statements express the low evaluation of women then current in almost all areas of life, Jesus for his part, knows no such animosities. 'Now, Jesus' more immediate and more extended environment was androcentric or patriarchal: it was charged with animosity. Jesus was free of animus. Jesus represents a great exception, indeed a unique exception, we might add, in view of what we said above. Jesus encounters women with spontaneous natural understanding in matter-of-fact acceptance, in natural partnership, with complete lack of any trace of resentment. This spontaneous natural acceptance is the diametric opposite of animosity. It was not least because of this attitude that Jesus was persecuted. It led to his ultimate fate.[36] Finally too we should stress Jesus' turning to children (see Mark 10:13-16). This too is a demonstrative sign that is intended to make clear the recognition of 'new value' which Jesus confers on man; for children in Jewish society had no value for their own sake.[37]

2.2.3. Normally the traits which we have just named are simply classified as products of the decisive factor of Jesus' 'compassionate love'. This is to diminish their significance too far. Jesus' attitude is a significant demonstration, to show that these very persons who are ignored, despised and defamed by society, have a right to recognition, to show that there is an inalienable dignity of man, a right to which also the 'sinner', the outcast, the criminal, are entitled. With his attitude Jesus is bearing witness to the fact that, as Kant puts it, he recognises man not as the 'means' but as the 'end' in itself, and that Jesus sees in each and every person the creature loved by God, and by seeing people in this light he is thereby honouring mankind in its humanity.[38] There is absolutely no distinction at this point between human rights and human dignity. At this juncture we should again stress how important it is that the women were naturally and fully accepted in the circle of Jesus' disciples, and quite certainly played a full and equal participatory decisive role. Even if Jesus' attitude cannot be reduced in the last resort to mere legal categories, since his motivation is the twin divine purpose—love and salvation—nevertheless one cannot avoid drawing the conclusion, and indeed for this very reason one is absolutely compelled to draw the conclusion, that such an attitude as demonstrated by Jesus tends quite decisively in a direction which leads to full recognition of human rights in Church and society. Put even more clearly: in particular a community which, like the Church, claims to be acting in the name of Jesus Christ, is compelled to follow his motivation and not only stand up for human rights in the external world, but has first of all to ensure that human rights are given top priority recognition and are practised in a convincing way within the Church's own sphere.

2.3. In the Pauline concept of the 'righteousness of God' (*dikaiosunê theou: iustitia dei*), the proclamation of Jesus is taken up by Paul once more and expanded. As E. Käsemann points out: 'The righteousness of God' refers to God taking back into the sphere of His Law the fallen world, whether it be in the promise or claim, in new creation, or forgiveness, or the possibility of our service. Käsemann further states that the Pauline doctrine of justification is to this extent nothing more than the theologically more precise variation of the earliest Christian proclamation of the supremacy of God the King as our eschatological salvation.[39]

2.3.1. It is not customary in traditional Catholic systematics, as compared with the Protestant tradition, to think on the basis of the Pauline doctrine of justification and use it to justify the Law. It is more usual to approach it by thinking in natural law categories. It is all the more important to take up the hint given us by the Pauline approach. Paul begins from the situation that man is a sinner and has therefore relinquished any right in the sight of God and that for man there exists no possibility, even through (observance of) the Mosaic Law, of accomplishing his own righteousness in the sight of God (cf. Rom. 1:18-3:19). According to Paul, this includes even the Law. Over against this, through Jesus Christ, in his death and resurrection, God has established his righteousness now outside the Law, 'since it is the same justice of God that comes through faith to everyone, Jew and pagan alike, who believes in Jesus Christ' (*Jerusalem Bible,* Rom. 3:22). This new righteousness is for the 'godless' person and for the person who is 'hostile to God' (Rom. 5:6-9), who through faith has this righteousness presented to him as an undeserved right, a right which cannot be earned either by 'works of the law' or by any legal ordinances or system. *Justificatio impii*—this basic recognition of the person alienated from God, recognition by God himself, theologically, must form the basis of a new understanding of justice and must surely validate inalienable human rights. A system of human rights will have as its prerequisite its 'divine quality' as 'righteousness of God through the faith of Jesus Christ' and such justice which remains 'unavailable for human disposal' will form the basis of all human rights. Such belief in the premise of divinely effected human rights is, in the Pauline view, at the roots of faith. Rights which are owed by a person to any other person, rights which people want to promise and guarantee to each other, are always problematical so long as they are not anchored in divine law as a whole. This divine law as a whole is not be be misunderstood as a speculative idea, it is an activity of God justifying men. This same *ius divinum*, God's justice, law and righteousness is thus, in NT terms, not a characteristic quality of God; it is not the legal legitimation of a legal system of justice, which one perhaps claims to be divine, it is, on the contrary, dynamically understood, the '*iustitia Dei non qua ipse iustus est, sed qua nos iustos facit*' as the Council of Trent (Sessio VI. *Decr. de iuistificatione.* Cap. 7) accurately formulates it.

This understanding of the 'righteousness of God' in the Pauline sense, goes far beyond normative human justice, far beyond any concept from jurisprudence defining justice and righteousness. Here righteousness is subsumed in divine love. 'What proves that God loves us is that Christ died for us while we were still sinners' (*Jerusalem Bible*, Rom. 5:8; cf. whole passage Rom. 5:6-11). The righteousness of God which makes men just is his love which brings them salvation, love made visible in the Cross of Christ. God's love and his will that men should attain salvation are universally applicable to all men, to the world, the cosmos, all history. What is involved is reconciliation of the world (to Christ) (see 2 Cor. 5:19), 'world-love' (John 3:16). For the believer in Jesus Christ, God's deed of salvation is a happening which concerns all mankind. God's love is all-encompassing. Just as the quality of being in the image of God, which was established in the Creation, is universal, so too salvation is universal, which God effected in Jesus Christ. *God wills justice for everyone, including justice for the sinner too.*

2.3.2. With this must be linked the perspectives of the chief commandment: to love God and one's neighbour. This commandment is likewise unrestricted and knows no limits to its human applicability. Essentially this commandment to love is nothing other than the imperative exactly corresponding to the biblical idea of God as the liberator-God, who expressly wills and effects salvation for man. God asks nothing else in return than that man should himself accept this universal purpose and adopt the will to salvation and the resolve to love, adopting them as his own intention.

2.3.3. How is love to be manifested in concrete situations in a world which is finite and variously fragmented? This love in concrete terms is the love shown in aid to those who need help. It is shown in justice and righteousness. 'Righteousness is the concretisation of the attitude described as love'.[41] It is clear that there can be no real contradiction between love and righteousness in the final analysis. Indeed there *must* be no contradiction, for love is manifested as the firm resolve to give the other person justice, and to give him assistance to secure the justice that is rightly his. Love is manifest and present where it is pure and not intent upon the subjugation of others, where it reveals as its purpose the freedom, independent maturity and full humanity of others. Love is the expression of the resolve that all people may lead a free human existence. Love cannot tolerate social injustice; it will campaign with full commitment for social justice and just conditions. This being so, active involvement to ensure human rights is not in contradiction to the Gospel, but it is rather a postulate which arises out of the heart of the Gospel, from the image of God we find in the Bible.

Translated by Alasdair Stewart

Notes

1. See various commentaries on Genesis, including, recently: C. Westermann 'Genesis', *BKAT* I, 1 (Neukirchen, 1974); especially excursus: 'Zur Auslegungsgeschichte von Gn. 1:26-27' pp. 203-214; G. Söhngen 'Die biblische Lehre von der Gottebenbildlichkeit des Menschen', in G. Söhngen *Die Einheit der Theologie: Gesammelte Abhandlungen, Aufsätze und Vorträge* (Munich 1952) pp. 173-211; F. Horst 'Der Mensch als Ebenbild Gottes in F Horst *Gottes Recht: Gesammelte Studien zum Recht im Alten Testament*, Theol. Bücherei, 12 (Munich 1971) pp. 222-234; H. Wilderberger, Article on '*saelaem*/Abbild' in *THAT* II, pp. 556-563.

2. One of the most important passages is *Bab. Talmud* Tractate Sanhedrin 56a-59a. See further Billerbeck *Kommentar zum N.T. aus Talmud und Midrasch* III, pp. 36-43, 126-133; A. Cohen *Le Talmud* (Paris 1976) p. 111.

3. See Billerbeck, III, 729; on the Apostles' decree cf. H. Conzelmann 'Die Apostelgeschichte' *H.N.T.* 7 (Tübingen 1963) p. 84 f.

4. On the concept of *philanthropia* see Luck, article in *Th. W.N.T.* 9, pp. 107-111. On the philosophical up-grading of the concept of *humanitas* in classical antiquity, see above all Cicero *De Officiis*, III 6, 27: 'Atque etiam si hoc natura praescribit, *ut homo homini, quicumque sit, ob eam ipsam causam, quod is homo sit,* consultum velit, necesse est secundum eandem naturam omnium utilitatem esse communem. Quod si ita est, una continemur omnes et eadem lege naturae, idque ipsum si ita est, certe violare alterum naturae lege prohibemur' ('And further, if nature ordains that one man shall desire to promote the interests of a fellow-man, *whoever he may be, just because he is a fellow-man*, then it follows, in accordance with that same nature, that there are interests that all men have in common. And if this is true, we are all subject to one and the same law of nature; and if this also is true, we are certainly forbidden by nature's law to wrong our neighbour'). (Loeb edition, pp. 292-295, trl. W. Miller)—H. Preisker *Neutestamentlich Zeitgeschichte* (Berlin 1937) p. 68 f.

5. Preisker *Zeitgeschichte* p. 68.

6. See Luck *Th.W.N.T.* 9, 109 f.

7. Philo *De Virtutibus (de hum)*. Cf. L. Cohn-P. Wendland *Philonis Alexandrini opera quae supersunt,* Vol. V (Berlin^2 1962) pp 266-335; de humanitate = sections 51-174, pp. 279-320; there is a German translation edited by Cohn-Heinemann-Adler-Theiler II (Berlin^2 1962) pp. 332-363; *Les oeuvres de Philon d'Alexandrie* eds. Arnaldez-Pouilloux-Mondésert, t. 26 *De Virtutibus* introduction and notes by R. Arnaldez, translation by P. Delobre-M. R. Servel-A. M. Verilhac (Paris 1962): (Translator's Note: Philo's works are conveniently available in 10 vols. in the Loeb series. An English translation of Philo—*On the Virtues* by F. Colson, is in Vol. VIII (Loeb Greek series, Vol. 341, 3rd impr. 1939) pp. 158-305, 440-450.)

8. Philo *De Virtutibus,* section 141: 'After this let those clever libellers continue, if they can, to accuse the nation of misanthropy and charge the laws with enjoining unsociable and unfriendly practices . . .' (F. Colson, p. 249).

9. Philo, section 66.

10. Philo, section 80

11. Philo, sections 82-87.
12. Philo, section 88.
13. Philo, section 89.
14. Philo, sections 90-94.
15. Philo, sections 97-101.
16. Philo, sections 102-104.
17. Philo, sections 105-108.
18. Philo, sections 109-120.
19. Philo, sections 121-124.
20. Philo, sections 125-147.
21. Philo, sections 148-160.
22. Philo, section 131. 'Read this law, you good and highly prized parents, and hide your faces for shame, you who ever breathe slaughter against your infants, who mount your wicked watch over them as they leave the womb, waiting to cast them away, you deadly enemies of the whole human race' (F. Colson, p. 243).
23. Philo, section 77.
24. Cf. Philo *Oeuvres* 26, p. 72, note 3.
25. Philo *De Virtutibus,* section 168.
26. Philo, sections 171-174.
27. Philo, sections 119-120.
28. Cf. N. Brox 'Die Pastoralbriefe' *RNT* 7 (Regensburg 1969) p. 306 ff.
29. Schillebeeckx *Jesus* 125; Merklein *Die Gottesherrschaft als Handlungsprinzip* pp. 31-35.
30. On Psalm 72, Cf. H. J. Kraus 'Psalmen' *BKAT* XV/1 (Neukirchen 1960), 493-500; according to Kraus, the King appears not only as source of justice but as saviour. He takes over the functions which in the Psalter are otherwise only exercised by Yahweh Himself (p. 498).
31. See H. Wildberger 'Jesaja' *BKAT* X/1, Jesaja 1-12 (Neukirchen 1972) pp. 436-462.
32. Cf. C. Westermann 'Das Buch Jesaja Kap. 40-66' *A.T.D.* 19 (Göttingen 1966) pp. 290-292.
33. Cf. P. Hoffman-V. Eid 'Jesus von Nazareth und eine christliche Moral' *Q.D.* 66 (Frieburg-Basel-Vienna 1975) p. 32: 'Jesus is evidently following O.T.-Judaic tradition; the reference to Isaiah 61:1 f. in the Beatitudes is clearly discernible.'
34. Cf. J. Blank 'Das Herrenmahl als Mitte der christlichen Gemeinde im Urchristentum' in Blank, etc. *Das Recht der Gemeinde auf Eucharistie. Die bedrohte Einheit von Wort und Sakrament* (Trier 1978) pp. 8-29.
35. H. Wolff *Jesus der Mann. Jesus in tiefenpsychologischer Sicht* (Stuttgart[3] 1978).
36. H. Wolff, *ibid.*, 82.
37. Cf. E. Neunhäusler *Anspruch und Antwort Gottes* (Dusseldorf 1962) p. 123 f.: 'In the child one saw the future adult, a being who would one day be capable of understanding the Torah. For only understanding of the Torah makes a man a grown-up mature adult.' (p. 135.)
38. I. Kant *Werke in sechs Bänden* edited by W. Weischedel, IV, *Schriften zur Ethik und Religionsphilosophie* (Darmstadt 1956), *Grundlegung zur Metaphysik*

der Sitten pp. 11-102: 'Act in such a way that you never use mankind, represented either by yourself or by another person, merely as a means, but always also regard that person as an end' (p. 61).

39. E. Käsemann 'An die Römer' *H.N.T.* 8a (Tübingen 1973), 26; Käsemann 'Gottesgerechtigkeit bei Paulus' in Käsemann *Exegetische Versuche und Besinnungen, 2* (Göttingen 1964) pp. 181-194.

40. Cf. H. Dombois *Das Recht der Gnade* (Witten 1961).

41. Preisker *Ethos* p. 79.

Bernard Plongeron

Anathema or Dialogue? Christian Reactions to Declarations of the Rights of Man in the United States and Europe in the Eighteenth Century

THE CHRISTIAN reaction: anathema or dialogue? The question will surprise many people who are already convinced that the Gospel and those basic texts, the American Declarations of 1776-1787 and the French Declaration of 1789 share, in some way, a common nature.

Others, better-informed, remember, nevertheless, the fulminations of the Catholic hierarchy against the Declaration of 1789, which they roundly declared to be a work of the devil and not of the Gospel. But, they may object, have we not moved on from the denunciation of the nineteenth century to the dialogue of the twentieth?

If, in spite of everything, we still insist on our question—anathema or dialogue?—it is because it remains historically relevant and also brings to light certain areas of confusion which still exist in the contemporary Christian struggle for the rights of man. Three such areas may be singled out for examination. The first concerns the methodological confusion which consists in treating as articles of faith, and thus as theological issues, rights which have been traditionally considered in the West as matters of public order. The second derives from the historical evidence: reactions in revolutionary Europe from 1789 to 1800 revealed some very complex attitudes among Catholics: sometimes they disagreed openly with the condemnation of the rights of man by a hierarchy which could not, on this score, guarantee the reaction of the Church as a whole. The third area of confusion, and not the least important, is, in effect, the reduction of the universal, basic rights of man: liberty, equality, fraternity—to the struggle for particular, specific freedoms, however essential or legitimate. This attitude became widespread after 1919, at a time when social and political rights had won increasing acceptance.

1. THE WESTERN TRADITION OF A DECLARATION OF RIGHTS FROM THE THIRTEENTH TO THE TWENTIETH CENTURY: ONE AND DIVISIBLE

Contrary to a commonly-held view, the French and American Declarations were neither spontaneously produced by the rationalism of the enlightenment, nor mere accidents in the course of Western civilisation. Among their predecessors must be mentioned *Magna Charta* (1215), the *Habeas Corpus Act* (1679) and the *Bill of Rights* (1689) which was completed, the same year, by the *Toleration Act,* which granted, (three years after the revocation of the *Edict of Nantes,* in France), freedom of worship to all, except Catholics and Unitarians. All of these were designed to restore peace to the country after major political upheavals. They still required in addition a long process of maturation, which was to be the work, not of the theologians but of philosophers, and in particular John Locke. In 1689 he published his two *Treatises of Civil Government,* which constituted a justification of the Revolution of 1688. By establishing a basis which was natural (and no longer political) and general (and no longer a matter of toleration with respect to particular freedoms) for liberty, Locke enabled the transition to the American Declarations to be made.

The dynamic quality of the form taken by these rights in America was definitively established by the Declaration of Independence of 1776: the right to life, liberty and the pursuit of happiness. It is worth noting this dynamic based on life, as typical of the 'American dream' and of its belief in the coming future of man, in the hope of a world to be built for the happiness of all. The French axiomatic system of liberty, equality and fraternity is more arid and still turned towards the past: the preamble to the Declaration of 1789 repeats four times the words 'no longer' in order to set the seal on the death certificate of the *ancien régime.*

Passing from the American Declaration to the French, therefore, we see not merely a more detailed version of a solemn affirmation of the natural and fundamental rights of man, but a change of perspective.

2. THE RECEPTION OF THE FRENCH AND AMERICAN DECLARATIONS AND CATHOLIC REACTIONS DURING THE AMERICAN REVOLUTION

The majority or minority status enjoyed by the Churches was the phenomenon which controlled the dialectic of anathema and dialogue.

When the argument of confessional majority or minority status coincided with theological positions, the Churches centred their consideration of the question of the fundamental rights of man on the issue of religious freedom.

It was, it seems, this approach that was to be adopted by those bishops who commented on the anathema pronounced by Pius VI in his brief *Quod Aliquantum* of March 10th 1791. Of the seventeen articles of the Declaration of 1789, the Pope only selected for comment articles 10 ('No man shall suffer disturbance for his opinions, even those on religion, so long as their expression does not disturb the public order by law established') and 11 ('The free communication of thought and opinion is one of the most cherished rights of man; all citizens may therefore speak, write and print freely, except that they must answer for the abuse of that freedom in those cases determined by law'). This did not involve 'unbridled freedom' as the 'papal brief' states, but rather, in the name of liberty of conscience (art. 10) the ending of the privileged status of the Catholic religion in France. Pius VI preferred to see it as a sinister conspiracy: 'This equality, this liberty, so highly exalted by the National Assembly, have then as their only result the overthrow of the Catholic religion, and that is why it has refused to declare it to be *predominant* in the realm, although it has always enjoyed this title.[1]

But when, after 1793, Catholics were forced to recognise the irreversible and expansionist progression of the 'immortal principles of 1789', they were to change their tactics. Rather than perpetuate an absolutely sterile denunciation of the Declaration of Rights, they preferred to claim for the Catholic religion the safeguards offered by article 10 on liberty of conscience.

Unlike their co-religionists in France, the Catholics of the new Batavian Republic had not been compelled, before experiencing the delights of the rights of man, to drink the cup of bitterness. The Catholics of the United Provinces were well aware of the religious persecution raging in France since 1792, and of the denunciation of the rights of man in *Quod Aliquantum*: the *émigré* French bishops who had settled particularly in Bois-le-Duc had often expounded this text to them. But what relevance did this have for them, an oppressed minority whose spirits could only be stirred by such words as 'rights', liberty, equality?

In fact, the new Batavian Republic proclaimed, on August 5th, 1796, the separation of Church and State. This hardly affected the Reformed Church, which was already based on the quasi-republican structure of the Calvinist congregations. By contrast, the Catholics immediately began to speak of their 'emancipation', a notion which, in other Christian states, was only applicable to Jews. All in all, the fortunate beneficiaries of the Declaration of Rights were the Catholics.

Was the Declaration of Rights to degenerate into that practical utilitarianism whose rallying cry could have been the remark falsely attributed to Louis Veuillot, in the nineteenth century, speaking to his liberal opponents: 'When we are in the minority, we demand freedom in the name of your principles; when in the majority, we refuse it to you in the name of ours'?[2] The Dutch example could give this impression, and apparently offers many points of similarity to the American situation.

Like their brethren in the United Provinces, the Catholic colonists, on the eve of independence, were in a minority in the thirteen colonies of North America. Indeed, they were a mere handful of farmers, swamped by the much larger Protestant community. This minority, even more despised than persecuted for their allegiance to popery were still waiting for the recognition of their civil rights quite as much as for the freedom to practise their religion openly. One can well understand their enthusiastic participation in the War of Independence, both against the king and, at the same time, against the 'established' Church of England, which practised its own additional oppression of the Catholic and dissenting Protestant minorities.

It is here that the originality of the attitude of the Maryland Catholics can be seen. They fought as Americans and as Catholics, but were sustained by the tradition of religious tolerance established by Lord Baltimore, who had founded the colony in the seventeenth century. This American-Catholic phenomenon in the tradition of Maryland was, moreover, given further significance by a family, the Carrolls, which was to play a leading part in the Constitution of the American States.

To what extent, however, did the position of the Catholics of Maryland reflect the 'spirit of 1776' which breathes through the Declaration of Independence? Was it not, in the final analysis, nearer to that attitude of mind based on 'Christian civilisation' in which a Europe which had its own theologico-political preconceptions was steeped?

3. 'CHRISTIAN CIVILISATION' VERSUS 'BIBLE COMMONWEALTH': THEOLOGICAL PRESUPPOSITIONS AND PATTERNS OF THOUGHT

It has often been stated that one reason for the Church's hostility to the principles of '89 was the fact that they formed a corpus of doctrine which was self-sufficient, since it was founded on reason, not revelation. The quite opposite attitude of the American Churches to these same philosophical presuppositions found in the Declaration of Independence may therefore appear astonishing. This must be accounted for by making a detailed comparison of two intellectual world-views which elaborated two political theologies displaying two contrary evaluations of man. One was the totalitarian vision of the integrality of Christian doctrine informed by the ideology of 'Christian civilisation'. It was opposed by the vision of the social compact between God and man, or the Puritan utopia which was democratic because it was based on the Bible: the 'Bible Commonwealth'.[3]

Was the Declaration of 1789 a challenge to the Catholic Church, or was it necessary for religious minds to consider it as such? Herein lies the whole problem of 'Christian civilisation'. When the counter-revolutionary apologists insisted so much on the status of the Catholic religion as 'predominant' (one may recall Duvoisin, in succession to Pius VI) it was not only to safeguard the position of the doctrine of divine right as specifically characteristic of Christianity, but also, and primarily, because only (the 'true') religion, or religious society, can complete and perfect the civil order, which by its nature is imperfect. For those men, there was no more possibility of the 'natural' without the 'social' than there was of the 'social' without the 'religious'. The first two orders can only find their political and metaphysical purpose in the third.

This inspired the lapidary formula of Pius XI in *Divini Redemptoris* (1937): 'Christian civilisation, the only truly human City'. As the principles of 1789 separated the political and the metaphysical there was, thereafter, a radical incompatibility between the Church and the Declaration of Rights, reflected in the constant, uniform teaching of Popes from Pius VII to Pius XII, in his Christmas radio message of 1944, on the problem of democracy. How, indeed, could it have been otherwise? It would have meant the ruin of the whole Augustinian vision of the Catholic West.

This involves a long historical perspective of which we shall only note the essentials, as seen in the four stages of the human condition defined by Saint Augustine: *ante peccatum, sub peccato, sub gratia, in gloria.* At the origin of Adamic man was that state of *ante peccatum,* which, with the coming of original sin, is revealed for sinful man in society, by a nostalgia for Paradise Lost. The state of *sub peccato* denies the myth of a pure innocence and the claims of the philosophers to speak of 'natural' rights. Man *sub peccato,* since he is only 'redeemed' by grace, has no rights: he has only 'duties towards God', as the catechisms of the nineteenth and twentieth centuries repeat. The emancipation of man in the name of rights dictated by reason is a political nonsense because it is a theological monstrosity (Duvoisin). It follows logically that man is subordinate to the divine order of which the Church is the custodian and interpreter. The Church, as the regime of 'Christian civilisation' cannot tolerate the claim that man has a future to build, or in other words a historicity, since that future lies behind him, in that original sin which he will have to atone for throughout his life, *sub gratia,* by faithfully fulfilling his 'duties' towards the Creator, the Sovereign Legislator who delegates subordinate power to popes and kings whom He has anointed. The anthropological vision of the Rights of Man and that of 'Christian civilisation' are thus poles apart. To say, for example, with H. Wattiaux[4] that *Divini Redemtoris* is 'the first papal declaration of the personal rights of man' is to accord scant importance to the 'thesis' of Christian civilisation which conditions it: 'Civil society and the individual human being owe their origin to God and are, by Him, mutually bestowed on each other; consequently, neither, therefore, may avoid their duties towards the other, nor deny, nor diminish, the rights of the other. It is God who has ordered this mutual relationship in its essential structure' (n. 33) . . . *sub peccato, sub gratia*!

It is just as incorrect to affirm that with 'Leo XIII, Catholic doctrine is reconciled with the rights of man': successive papal pronouncements prove it. To begin with, one would have to deny *Immortale Dei* (1885) on the Christian constitution of societies, which served as a point of reference for Pius XII in his 1944 radio message. It is true that *Rerum Novarum* did make some contribution to an increased respect for the poor and the workers and that 'from this persistent effort, a new right was born, quite unknown in the previous century, guaranteeing to workers respect for their sacred rights derived from their dignity as men and as Christians', as Pius XI recalled in *Quadragesimo Anno* (1931) nr. 30.[5]

But it was still a matter of defending particular freedoms—important ones, no doubt—necessitated by the *hypothesis* of the secularised society of the industrial age; this society could not be absorbed into the *thesis* of a Christian society based on duties towards God and opposed to the concept of universal, basic, natural rights of a mankind which had come of age and was master of its historical destiny.

Leo XIII adopted this strategy of the hypothesis which had been pursued by social and liberal Catholics (e.g., *Lamennais*). These Catholics proclaimed in 1877, following A. de Mun: 'Let us oppose the *Declaration of the Rights of Man* which served as a basis for the Revolution, and proclaim the *Rights of God,* which must be the foundation of the counter-revolution. Ignorance or forgetfulness of these is the real cause of the evil which is leading modern society to its ruin.'

Such indeed was the *thesis* of 'Christian civilisation'. . . defended by the Abbé Grégorie in 1789 before the Constituent Assembly!

The theological presuppositions and mental attitudes which inspired the American 'spirit of 1776' were quite different. The fundamental difference between 'Christian civilisation' and 'Bible Commonwealth' stems from the fact that the Puritans, the future Dissenters, made no distinction between metaphysical and political freedom. For them, Biblical certainties were mystical, and indeed practical, truths. Burke was aware of this when he declared to the Commons that their 'jealousy of all that looks like absolute government' should not 'be sought for so much in their religious convictions as in their history'.

This was a twofold allusion by Burke to the 'Mayflower Compact' of 1620 and to the congregationalist structure of the Dissenting Churches, illustrated by the Puritan preacher *par excellence,* Cotton Mather: 'We came here because we would have our posterity settled under the pure and full dispensation of the Gospel, defended by rulers that should be of ourselves'. That is to say, defended against the theologico-political absolutism of James I of England and the clerical despotism of the 'Established' Church, the living contradiction of that Bible from which the Dissenters naturally drew their civil as well as their religious beliefs. Before their departure from England, the Mayflower Pilgrims had sworn: 'We (. . .) do by these presents, solemnly and mutually, in the presence of God and of one another, covenant and combine ourselves together into a civil body politic, for our better ordering and preservation, and furtherance of the ends aforesaid'. Four times, in this document, the expression 'we covenant' is repeated. This *covenant,* or contract, was reflected in the Church structures which they established for themselves.

The concept of the Church was to refer, not to a national, provincial or diocesan body, but rather to a congregation, which recognised no other authority save that of God Himself. An essential principle, since this refusal to acknowledge any external authority over the gathered community, the *ecclesia,* contained the seeds of a certain democratic conception, implying a government of the group by the group, and a considerable possibility of self-determination. It is evident that there existed also in congregationalism the basis of a certain kind of federalism, since each Church, although it was autonomous, had to establish a bond of association, of *fellowship,* with the other Churches, so that the whole formed a 'commonwealth' based on the Word of God.

In the Calvinist tradition, everyone believed 'that it is conscience, and not the power of man, which will bring us to seek the kingdom of God'. The fact remains that the main principle of this grand adventure was that of a Covenant theology which gave responsibility to each man and institution (instead of treating them as minors as in 'Christian civilisation'). This responsibility was to lead to *self-government* and *free consent.* Throughout the seventeenth and early eighteenth centuries Puritan sermons ceaselessly refined this theology of the contract: 'The general will of the regenerate (the Puritans themselves) bound by the social compact projects and continues the will of God in the State', declared, among others, John Winthrop,[6] because society is the result of a free contract between its citizens, but once it is established this free society takes on a sacred character, the seal of God: woe to the man who would seek to alter it! There was thus a kind of immediate relationship between the natural and the divine (a horrifying idea for the 'redeemed' man of 'Christian civilisation') which inspired Hamilton to write these famous words in 1775: 'The sacred rights of mankind are not to be rummaged for, among old parchments, or musty records. They are written, as with a sun beam, in the whole *volume* of human nature, by the hand of the divinity itself; and can never be erased or obscured by mortal power.' Of course, this direct relationship of the natural and the divine is mediated through three covenants: the first is with God Himself, the second binds men to each other in the framework of the Church, and the third links them to the State as such. Also, of course, in the period between the pure Biblical utopia, the 'New heaven and the new earth' of the seventeenth century, and the enthusiasm of the young Hamilton for 'rights', one must take account of a secularisation of thought which tempers the mythology of the Promised Land and the New Jerusalem in the Declaration of Independence.

The religion of Jefferson and the Virginians as revealed in the Philadelphia Convention, from which the American Constitution was to emerge, is a matter of some debate and will long continue to be so. Nevertheless, the fact remains that the Americans, by the mouth of Jefferson in his second inaugural address, proclaimed: 'Europe is Egypt; America, the Promised Land. God has led His people to establish a new social order which shall also be revealed to all nations'. Perhaps, first of all, because the Americans had very early received the revelation that 'liberties are of the gift of God', as Jefferson also said, in his *Notes on Virginia,* and that therefore they might not be violated by divine right nor be used by popular absolutism in the name of a demagogic liberalism which had been explicitly exorcised by the American Constitution. But the American revelation to other nations is much more closely concerned with the proclamation of the right to life. Life ceases to be human without liberty and equality. Through life, man creates society, instead of being created by it. In the name of life, which is the gift of God, rights are placed beyond discussion. They are not at the end of history, they begin history and direct its course in a dynamic movement in which are combined man's ambition, his pursuit of happiness, and the hope of a new Heaven . . . on a new earth.

The language of theological hope should forever exclude the twofold language of anathema and dialogue. This is the very lesson of History itself, recalled by A. Latreille, the historian of the Catholic Church and the French Revolution: 'The Churches have undergone the apprenticeship of events, and of all that these events involve; and they have learned, in particular, definitively, that in crises of the magnitude of the one which has occurred since the advent of Nazism (. . .) it is incumbent on those religious forces which aspire to exercise a certain moral authority on public opinion to defend, in a completely open-minded and liberal way, not only religious liberty (as Catholics have often declared, and which has almost always meant their own liberty), but the rights of man. . . .'[7] And even on this specific issue of religious freedom, there is a real theological task which remains to be undertaken, if we may judge by certain 'ecumenical' expressions of dissatisfaction. Thus Pastor Hébert Roux tells of his visit to Rome to speak to a group of French bishops during the discussion by the Council of the document *Dignitatis humanae.* 'It is not enough', he pointed out to them, 'to say that the "principle" of the natural right to religious freedom "does not contradict" the truth of the Gospel, but it is necessary to show the close correlation in the Gospel itself (i.e., starting out from the person and work of Christ) between truth as the content of the Faith and the freedom of man's conscience. . . .'

The bishops recognised that they found some difficulty in entering into this mode of thought, accustomed as they were to referring back to the teaching of the *magisterium*.[8] This is an obvious proof that our question remains valid, the question of the attitudes of mind of which we have sought here, very rapidly, to show the different types of approach, as a contribution to a problem which remains, in our view, completely unresolved. Is a theology of freedom only the sum of individual freedoms—as nineteenth century liberal Catholics believed—or is it something other? If the latter is true, the theologian can make progress only in the light of history, as he attempts to establish, once and for all, an unequivocal and stimulating language for each individual conscience.

Translated by Lawrence Ginn

Notes

1. Underlined in the original Latin.
2. Quoted by H. Madelin 'La liberté religieuse et la sphère du politique. Pour l'intelligence de la déclaration *Dignitatis Humanae Personae Nouv. Revue Théol.,* 97, no. 2, (1975) pp. 110-126; p. 125.
3. B. Plongeron, *Théologie et Politique au siècle des Lumières* 1770-1820, (Geneva, Droz 1973) pp. 318-326.
4. H. Wattiaux 'Statut des interventions du Magistère relatives aux droits de l'homme' *Nouv. Rév. Théol.,* 98/9, (1976) p. 802-3.
5. The historian should, however, note that the right to work was proclaimed for the first time in the French Constitution of 1793, art. 21, by virtue of the principle that 'state aid to the needy is a sacred obligation'.
6. Michael McGiffert (ed.) *Puritanism and the American Experience* (Mass. 1964).
7. In *Eglises et chrétiens dans la IIe Guerre mondiale* (Lyon 1978) p. 362-363.
8. Hébert Roux *De la désunion vers la communion. Un itinéraire pastoral et oecuménique* (Paris 1978) p. 225-226.

PART II

The Theology

Charles Wackenheim

The Theological Meaning of the Rights of Man

'BY VIRTUE of the Gospel entrusted to her, the Church proclaims the rights of man (*iura hominum*); she recognises and highly values the contemporary dynamism which is giving a new impetus to these rights everywhere.' This statement by Vatican II (*Gaudium et spes,* section 41, 3) raises at least two questions: In the language of the Council what does the expression *iura hominum* embrace? How is the current proclamation linked to the Gospel?

1. RECENT TEACHING BY THE MAGISTERIUM

On the first point we are referred back to the study of the two texts which take up in some detail the theme of the rights of man, i.e., sections 25-31 of *Gaudium et spes* and the declaration on religious freedom *Dignitatis humanae*. The pastoral constitution evokes 'the outstanding worth of man, who is the head of all things and whose rights and duties are universal and inviolable'. In the same passage the Council quotes the right to food, clothing, housing, the right to choose one's livelihood freely and to create a family, the right to education, work, reputation, respect, adequate news service, the right to act according to one's own conscience, the right to privacy and freedom, including religious freedom. The preface to the declaration *Dignitatis humanae* expresses its intention to develop the doctrine of the most recent sovereign Pontiffs on the inviolable rights of man. The Council refers in particular to the Encyclical of Pius XI *Mit brennender Sorge* (14th March 1937), to the messages of Pius XII for Christmas 1942 and 1944, finally to the Encyclical *Pacem in terris* of John XXIII, published 11th April 1963.

It is fair to think that in talking of the rights of man, the Council is implicitly appealing to *Pacem in terris.* In its first part this document does indeed provide a 'charter of the rights and responsibilities of man', which affirms many rights relating to his physical, moral and cultural life, to his economic, social and civic rights as well as to the corresponding responsibilities. But, in its turn, the spiritual testament of John XXIII indicates an obvious link with the *Universal Declaration of the Rights of Man,* promulgated on 10th December 1948 by the General Assembly of the United Nations. In the doctrine of *Pacem in terris* and indirectly in that of Vatican II, which drew its inspiration from it, should we see a sort of ecclesiastical guarantee of the United Nations text? In fact John XXIII and the Council's statement does not correspond exactly with the United Nations', as the particular inspiration is different.

Let us define exactly what is the peculiar basis of the conception of the rights of man advocated by the Catholic *magisterium.* According to the declaration on religious freedom, the dignity of man is known 'thanks to the revealed word of God and to reason itself'.[2] In *Gaudium et spes,* the Council affirms that 'all men, endowed with a rational soul and created in the image of God, share the same nature and the same origin; all, redeemed by Christ, enjoy the same calling and divine destiny. Their fundamental equality must therefore be increasingly acknowledged' (section 29, 1). This double argument—metaphysical and theological—is already visible in *Pacem in terris.* However, John XXIII is more insistent than Vatican II on the 'natural' foundation of his charter. 'The principles we have just set out', he writes in the fifth section of *Pacem in terris* 'are based on the very requirements of human nature and most often belong to the realm of natural law'.

What is to be understood by 'human nature' and by 'natural law'? Does Revelation always confirm the insights of reason? If tensions and conflicts occur, to what can we appeal to set the limits of the debate and what are the criteria? If the texts of the *magisterium* do not tackle this type of problem, the theologian nevertheless has to for the reasons set out below.

2. THEORY AND PRACTICE WITHIN THE CHURCH

There is no question within the limits of this article of retracing the history of Church practice which has more than once violated human freedom and dignity. What is important to notice is that we are faced not with passing incidents but with real structural change.

Now the politico-religious theory which has held sway in the Roman Church for a millenium and a half has not yet ceased to have its effects. Read again, for example, Vatican II's declaration on religious freedom promulgated on 7th December 1965. It is difficult today to understand why there had to be such a long document—and such laborious initial discussions—before enunciating a principle which had figured in all declarations of the rights of man since the eighteenth century. This principle is formulated in particularly relevant terms in *Dignitatis humanae*: 'The Vatican Council declares that man has a right to religious freedom. The nature of this freedom is that all men should be exempt from all constraint exercised by individuals, social groups or any human power, so that no-one is forced to act against his conscience in a religious matter or prevented from acting according to his conscience.' This confirms the substance of Article 10 of the *Declaration of the Rights of Man and of the Citizen* (26th August 1789), of Article 18 of the *Universal Declaration of the Rights of Man* (10th December 1948) and of Article 9 of the *European Convention for the protection of the Rights of Man and of Fundamental Freedoms* (4th November 1950). How does one then explain Vatican II's multiplication of rhetorical warnings, restrictions and equivocal formulae? The text declares categorically that 'all men are constrained to seek the truth particularly as it concerns God and his Church, to embrace it and be faithful to it once known'; that 'the freedom with which the only son of God has endowed the Church is sacred'; so that 'those who battle against it are acting against the will of God'; finally that 'by the will of Christ the Catholic Church is teacher of the truth', its function being 'to express and teach with authenticity the truth which is the Christ, and at the same time to declare and confirm by virtue of its authority, the moral principles derived from man's very nature' (section 14). To put it another way, the right to religious freedom is founded on the nature of man as interpreted by the Church's *magisterium*. In this way man's inalienable right is transformed into an obligation to belong to the Catholic Church!

In reality the problems of Vatican II have their roots in a deviation of Christian theology dating from the second half of the fourth century. At a time when authors such as Tertullian, Lactantius and Hilary of Poitiers were echoing the Gospel charter of freedom of conscience, from Firmicus Maternus on there were apologists of developing 'Christendom' and of violence to enforce doctrinal orthodoxy. Confusing offences of opinion and crimes against the common law, Augustine himself justifies recourse to the arm of the state in his struggle against the Donatists. Famous bishops of the period, such as Martin of Tours and Ambrose of Milan, refused to sanction such methods, but Pope Leo I (440-461) was to approve the execution in 385 of the heretic Priscillian. The mediaeval Inquisition was present in bud in this deadly association of Church and state. From then on, any attack on the unity of the faith would be seen as an attack on the social and political order.

The third and fourth Lateran Councils (1179 and 1215) heap privileges

on those who fight heresy, sword in hand. In calling for a Crusade against the Albigenses, Innocent III compared religious dissent to high treason. The legal basis of the Inquisition was laid by Pope Gregory IX and the Emperor Frederick II. By the Bull *Ad exstirpanda* (1252) Innocent IV advocated torture in the interrogation of suspects. The thirteenth-century theologians fall in line with the secular authorities in justifying this procedure. In Thomas Aquinas' writings, appealing to Augustine on this point, remarks such as this can be read: '(Heretics and apostates) must be forced, even physically (*sunt etiam corporaliter compellendi*), to honour their promises and to maintain what they accepted once and for all.' (*Summa Theologica,* 2a. 2ae., q.10, a.8; cf. q.11, a.4).

Why recall these facts and these texts from an earlier period? Has the page not finally been turned since the Church has ceased to link its fate to that of the temporal power? Certainly physical torture is no longer practised and happily dissidents escape the stake. But the current procedure of the 'Congregation for the teaching of the faith'—the contemporary heir of the holy congregation of the Inquisition—at several points contradicts the rights of man as they are proclaimed by the majority of states. For instance Article 10 of the *Universal Declaration* (1948) and Article 6 of the *European Convention* (1959) demand public legal debates, whereas the Roman regulations enforce secrecy.

This brief summary leads me to formulate the following hypothesis. The message of Jesus and of the primitive Church helped to give men a powerful awareness of their true dignity. During the first three centuries of the Christian era, the Church ceaselessly asserted the rights of man and this in the face of the claims of the imperial power. After 313, the need for the cohesion and survival of human institutions took precedence over the proclamation of 'the truth that makes men free' (Jn. 8:32). Once she gained the social and cultural leadership of the West, the Roman Church espoused as a matter of course the ideology of the established order. From this point of view the claim for individual rights necessarily appeared subversive. Barely a century before Vatican II, Pius IX could condemn out of hand a proposition like this: 'Any man is free to embrace and profess the religion which the light of reason has led him to judge to be the true one' (*Syllabus,* 1864, no. 15, DZS 2915). To explain the contradiction between this doctrine and that of *Pacem in terris* and *Dignitatis humanae* it is not enough to invoke the Papacy's legitimate reaction against the militant liberalism of the nineteenth century. The language of anathema was literally enforced on a Church which was the prisoner of the papal states and the guardian of a Christendom under threat. It is not surprising that since the Renaissance and the Aufklärung the affirmation and the defence of liberties should have encountered the hostility of the established Church.

3. ELEMENTS OF A THEOLOGICAL CRITIQUE

Learning from the past, we must now take up our position as Christians *vis-à-vis* the contemporary movement for the rights of man. Now this is practically unexplored territory.

We must begin by acknowledging the debt that the Christian world owes to all those individuals and groups who are at the root of the various 'declarations'. Many of these pioneers were not Christians, and some of them were forced to oppose the Churches in order to gain victory for their ideals. Even if we can distinguish the spirit and breath of the Gospel in their texts, we must avoid taking them over word for word. The Christian faith has an aim, the possession of which enables us progressively to discern the concrete demands of human dignity. Now, in this task of elucidation, each man receives from others as much as he can give them. It seems obvious that the first section of the declaration *Dignitatis humanae* (sections 2-8), substantially reproduces the arguments of the eighteenth-century philosophers in favour of tolerance. The Council would have gained in stature by acknowledging this openly. In the same way it would be good for us to admit that Christians were not amongst the most determined enemies of slavery and torture.

In order to realise what we owe others, we do not need to construct a theory of 'natural law'. In fact Catholic writers have difficulty in avoiding the temptation of claiming the monopoly of genuine interpretation in this field. It is the attribute of the 'natural' man specifically not to define himself by terms of reference which are foreign to him. Non-Christians who from now on make up eighty per cent of mankind, make pronouncements on the rights of man without any reference at all to the idea held by such and such a Church. As Christians we believe that all men, created in the image of God (Gen. 1:26-27), are called to put on 'the new man' (Eph. 2:15 and 4:24; Col. 3:10). For the disciple of Jesus, there is neither 'Jew nor Greek, bond nor free, male nor female' (Gal. 3:28). We believe that the spirit of God moves in the heart of every man, as the episode of the centurion Cornelius (Acts 10), amongst others, bears witness. According to Vatican II 'it is not uncommon that the Holy Spirit precedes the action of those who have the responsibility of the Church' (*Ad gentes,* 29). So, the compassion we feel towards all defenders of the rights of man rests on a common destiny, whose ultimate direction is revealed by the Christ himself. It is because it is modelled on the triune God that the dignity of the individual is a source of responsibilities as well as privileges.

This is what constantly moves us to denounce the fatal trap of individualism. As we know, this complaint was often made of the French declaration of the rights of man and of the citizen (1789). But all similar texts are open to the same accusation. Here the theologian can begin by adapting, up to a certain point, the Marxist criticism of the 'liberal' conception of the rights of man. In an article on the Jewish question (1843-1844), Karl Marx analyses the distinction between man and citizen which was consecrated by the French Revolution. Now, according to Marx, bourgeois society has codified and magnified the rights of the individual. Liberty is only each man's right to manage his private interests; equality is the right granted to all selfishly to enjoy the right of property; as for security, it is identified with the police guarantee with which society protects the rights of the individual. All 1789's work amounts finally to a sordid apology for bourgeois selfishness. 'None of the so-called rights of man', wrote Marx, 'goes beyond the selfish individual (. . .), turned in on himself, on his private interest and (. . .) separated from his social being' (MEGA 1, 1/1, p. 595). Of course the Christian does not share the Marxist conception of the 'social being' of man. The logic of the Gospel compels him to lend his voice *first of all* to those of his brothers who cannot succeed in making themselves heard: peoples of the Third World, exiles and immigrants, victims of economic exploitation, the handicapped, the ideological dissidents and all the oppressed. Within his Church, each man will seek to have the rights of the individual scrupulously respected. Thus the Roman Church must renounce the inflexible severity, itself the response to an indefensible legalism, which it shows towards divorced people who have remarried.

Moreover it is also the Christian's duty to be concerned about the indefeasible rights of the as yet unborn. For eschatology is also concerned about the earthly future of the human race. What sort of world are we preparing for future generations? Will industrial civilisation not take away their right to a 'human' existence? Add to this that concern for the future implies a new approach to the relationship between man and his environment. Not that nature must be considered subject to 'rights'; but the rights of man have ecological effects the extent of which we are just beginning to realise. The Biblical view of Creation conceived as cosmos provides conscience with a horizon which is totally lacking in our modern declarations of the rights of man.

4. FROM RIGHT TO RESPONSIBILITY

There is another fact which invites the theologian to be critically vigilant: that is the cultural relativity of the various theories of the rights of man. Different forms of consensus are reached in Western countries from those in socialist states and in the Third World. The result of this is that the 'declarations' already published are continually being amended and added to. Now it may be that the elaboration of new 'rights' provides an alibi for a policy which is harmful to such and such a category of specific individuals. 'The Sabbath was made for man, and not man for the Sabbath' (Mk. 2:27). What really matters is not the codification of abstract principles, but the fate of beings of flesh and blood who make up today and tomorrow's humanity. The rights of man are daily violated by states who have undertaken to respect them. What is worse, it can happen that those in power establish hierarchies and distinctions between 'rights of man' which justify their political plans. Instinctively Christians should therefore be in the forefront of those who denounce such manoeuvres and affirm the right of citizens to resist. As Christians, we should remind men in season and out of season that the dignity of the individual is more important than the collective interest and that the crimes committed in the name of the welfare of the state are no less to be condemned.

Thus one begins to wonder if there is not a sort of distortion between the central aim of the New Testament and the humanist ideal underlying the declarations of the rights of man. It seems indeed that the latter claim an increasing number of privileges for the individual whereas the Gospel kerygma pledges the individual to renounce even his legitimate rights. The disciple of Jesus is called to be reconciled with his adversary (Mt. 5:25), to let himself be struck on both cheeks (Mt. 5:39), to do good to those who hate him (Lk. 6:27), not to judge others (Rom. 2:1), but to forgive 'up to seventy times seven' (Mt. 18:22). The Christian life appears as the place where men freely gamble on love, thus following and imitating Jesus of Nazareth.

The Gospel of the beatitudes substitutes the idea of responsibility for that of right, i.e., the awareness of having to 'respond' without limit to the free gift of God. It is certainly not a question of humiliating justice in the name of love. It is on the contrary the unlimited sense of responsibility which grants their true basis to justice and right. 'As responsible men' Christians will fight for respect for the rights of man, but they will not be satisfied with restoring the legal order which has been violated. For the second commandment is like the first (Mt. 22:39), so that no-one can claim to love God if he hates his brother (I Jn. 4:20). From now on, the same attitude is required towards God and towards all men without exception. In making brotherly love the touchstone of the love of God, Jesus recognises in the creature a greatness which makes him like the Creator. Now the latter, as revealed by Jesus, has no 'rights' to assert: it is absurd to imply that to promote the dignity of man amounts to insulting the rights of God.

The synoptic writers report a saying of Jesus which defines the heart of every theological criticism of the rights of man: 'If any man would follow me, let him take up his cross and follow me' (Mk. 8:34; cf. Mt. 16:24 and Lk. 9:23). Taking up one's cross means to strip oneself of one's interests, fame, even one's life—in the manner of him who 'humbled himself to death, even death on a cross' (Phil. 2:7-8). This deliberate kenosis is at the opposite extreme from masochism and all forms of narcissism, as it is the way towards the 'Other'. By renouncing his 'rights', Jesus demonstrated a liberty capable of disarming contempt and hatred (cf. Eph. 2:16). By freely renouncing our individual advantages, we shall all the more respect every man's fundamental right to be welcomed and loved for himself.

Translated by Jean Rutherford

Stephan H. P. Pfürtner

Human Rights in Christian Ethics

1. ARE HUMAN RIGHTS A SUBJECT FOR CHRISTIAN ETHICS?

1.1. Today we hear a great deal of talk about human rights. Perhaps so many people are talking about them that the phrase is threatening to become a cliché. Or perhaps we are tired of hearing the words at all. Do Christian ethics now have to talk about human rights as well? It is true that recently human rights have increasingly become a theme for the Churches. This was by no means always the case. So why is it so today? Not, surely, because the Churches and the theologians want to be on the spot whenever society is moved by some moral passion, and especially if the emotion is provoked by forces outside the Church?

Whether we are tired of the phrase or not—whether it is a cliché or not—and even if we are suspected of simply conforming to the fashion—none of this must be the determining factor. The cause of human rights itself is inescapable and compelling. Anyone who had his eyes open cannot run away from it. Anyone who has a heart to feel is bound to be captured by it—unless he simply despairs of seeing human rights enforced. Only the cynic shrugs off their claim. Christians and the Church would have to become completely deaf to their God's message of loving-kindness towards men and his promise of peace, if they failed to allow themselves to be touched by what is at stake in human rights.

1.2. What Christian ethics has to concern itself about here is inescapable. *The violation of human rights is plain to everyone wherever men are reduced by other men to humiliated, enslaved, forsaken or despised people.* It was because of the men and women who were dehumanised in this way that Karl Marx set up his categorical imperative for the alteration of social conditions.[1] The major churches have only been committed to this battle in recent years. They were not originally involved in the development of human rights. They even behaved, refused to do so, or remained detached. But today they too believe that they are being challenged. This change of thinking and practical effort on the part of the churches gives rise to a number of problems; and the solution of these problems is certainly one of the tasks of Christian ethics.

2. HUMAN RIGHTS AS A CHALLENGE TO ECUMENCIAL ETHICS

2.1. First of all, it must be stressed that we have to deal with 'ethics' in many senses.[2] For the first and most important thing is that the ethics of human rights should be put into effect. What is at stake, therefore, is people's views about human rights, their attitude towards them, and the reality of human rights, as well as humane relationships, (ethics as content). But it is also a matter of the rightness of the whole complex of understanding and language in which this ethos is communicated. Christian ethics must therefore become a practical theory of human rights (must help to give meaning content to ethics). Finally, the Christian ethics of human rights as doctrinal and linguistic system must face up to a critical examination. (Ethics as object language must itself be the object of examination.) It must allow itself to be challenged as meta-ethics.

2.2. This interpretation of the term is of considerable importance. The last meaning given to the word is linked, for example, with the demand that Christian ethics *should ideally be judged by the principle of humanity before the tribunal of conscience,* which demands responsibility for people as people, over and above all the different religions and cultures. It is no longer enough to think solely in terms of our own religious system or our own religious group. However Christian ethics may be motivated by its theological presuppositions here, it must make itself comprehensible to everyone in its arguments and must consequently subject itself to a rational check on its general comprehensibility.

From this, it is not difficult to see why theologically motivated ethics, when they touch on human rights, cannot be adequately expressed and realised in social terms if they spring from individual ecclesiastical traditions or creeds. Of course the individual churches must face up to the task that has to be mastered in the light of their own historical, institutional and theological presuppositions. But they must do so with their eyes fixed on the overriding goal of a humanity promised by the Gospel of Christ. If it is only for the sake of making this humanity credible in the eyes of the public, they cannot pursue any ethical theory and practice which will be closed towards—let alone hostile to—the other churches.

Consequently we can only talk adequately about human rights in *Christian* ethics. It is not enough to start from the Catholic tradition, for example, or from the Protestant one. The Church's efforts on behalf of human rights categorically demand ecumenicity in the universal sense—ecumenicity with all the people who are concerned about a more humane world, and with all the institutions, social systems and religions which are committed to that purpose.[3] In this way the openness of churches and Christians to one another, and Christianity's openness to all the forces in society that are willing to work for a more humane world, becomes *the methodological and practical condition of the new Christian social ethic in whose midst human rights and the realisation of those rights must stand.* This ethic must be conceived universally and ecumenically, both doctrinally (as a doctrine of theory and practice) and practically. Otherwise it cannot be achieved at all.

2.3. The corollary of this is an important potential gain. If the bringing in of human rights succeeds in the sense we have described, then *the churches have here a new framework for their orientation towards the whole of society, as well as a context in which they can communicate practically with that society.* Christians and the churches can test the implementation of their social responsibility against their exertions for human rights, though they must certainly also allow themselves to be scrutinised critically by those rights. And these can help Christians and the churches to scrutinise the legitimation of the use of power by state and society.[4] Human rights would bind together all the people who are struggling on their behalf into a community of mind and action, beyond all the limitations of individual institutions. In this respect Christians and the churches would co-operate constructively to build a future world community. At the same time they would make their own contribution to counteracting the ever-new temptation towards isolation between religion and society. We must therefore call the ethics of human rights the ethics of the open society; and we must develop them accordingly.

3. HUMAN RIGHTS—A CALL TO REFORM AND A CHANCE FOR THE FURTHER DEVELOPMENT OF CHRISTIAN ETHICS

Christian self-understanding—or simply human self-understanding—demands exertion on behalf of the fundamental rights of man. That is why we said that we needed no further legitimation for calling human rights a subject of central importance for Christians and the churches (1.1.). If this is the case, then *we have to explain why theology and the Church have* only adopted the cause of human rights quite recently. Was it the modern term it lacked, or concern with the reality? What were the reasons for the one or the other, or for both? We do not have to settle these questions only out of historical curiosity or masochistic self-criticism. The answers are essential for the churches', or for Christian, orientation towards the present and the future. We must have this goal in mind when considering the matter theologically.

3.1. Let us begin with the phrase itself. The term 'human rights' has not been part of the churches' vocabulary for very long. Earlier, it was used as little in the churches' proclamation as in Christian (social) ethic. *Linguistic research would have to follow up this fact and its hermeneutical interpretation, as well as its implications for social criticism, in more detail.* Here we can only offer a few indications.

Let us look first at the linguistic context of Roman Catholicism. 'Human rights' were implicit in the 'natural rights of men and women' which Leo XIII asserted—for example in his encyclical on social justice *Rerum novarum* (1891).[5] But at that time the Pope shrank from using the phrase itself. He kept to the language stamped by Catholic thinking, which was in terms of natural law. And succeeding popes largely followed him in this respect. It was John XXIII who made the breakthrough for the first time, with his encyclical *Pacem in terris* (1963).[6] Even though he was careful not to break loose from the context of speech and thinking belonging to his own Church tradition, he none the less unmistakeably entered the territory of the modern development of human rights, which took place outside the Church. He called the declaration on human rights made by the United Nations in 1948 'an act of the greatest importance',[7] numbering it among 'the signs of the times'.[8] *Pacem in terris* was therefore termed 'the first declaration on human rights made by papal authority'.[9] Vatican II took up the theme of 'iura hominum' in its documents. But it was Paul VI who perhaps first used the phrase 'human rights' without worrying about earlier doctrinal repudiations of it.[10] The language of the ethical systems of the theologians can hardly have been more far-reaching in Catholicism. Isolated theological discussions occasionally anticipated the Church's 'official' linguistic development.

In Protestantism the encounter with the human-rights movement in society naturally took place under different systematic ecclesiastical and theological conditions from those of Catholicism. But we should probably not be wrong if we guessed that the linguistic discovery of the subject of human rights was made for the first time when the subject itself forced its way into Protestant consciousness—at the opening conference of the World Council of Churches in Amsterdam in 1948.[11] Before that, human rights were not a central theme in Protestant ethics either. And in German-speaking countries they are probably, largely speaking, not a central topic even today. Spot-checks in systematic work on theological ethics (in Helmut Thielicke[12] or Walter Kreck,[13] for example, or in Heinz-Horst Schrey's survey[14]) confirm this conjecture. Wolfgang Huber and Heinz Eduard Tödt, at all events, talk about the 'traditional detachment of German Protestantism with regard to human rights',[15] instancing cases to show how this detachment only began to change after the 1948 conference in Amsterdam.

3.2. *Does the lack of linguistic and doctrinal context reflect the Churches' lack of concern with the whole question of human rights*? This question is more important than the question about terms. Here too clarification calls for considerable historical research. But we can probably apply a double viewpoint.

On the one hand, it would be an untenable and unhistorical generalisation if we were to maintain that in the past theology and the churches were totally unmoved by human rights as a motivating force. *In some respects the cause of human rights was grasped by Christianity under different terminology*. It is sufficient confirmation of this statement to point to the practice of ministering love among the poor, the sick, the old and the imprisoned to which individuals, groups, orders or other charistmatic movements in the Church were continually driven by the spirit of the Gospel. If this concern had not existed—if, that is to say, Christianity had really passed by on the other side of the misery and injustice in the world—it would have betrayed the cause of the Gospel. Contrariwise, it was guilty in this matter to the degree in which it remained untouched.

This brings us to the other side, which must be clearly stated. *The Church and theology have, in important contexts, lost sight of not only the term but also the fact of human rights, as this impinges upon us in our era.* It only slowly became clear to them that what was at stake here was the both fundamental and simple cause of man as man—man in his humanity—man in his dignity—man in his right to live as man among his fellows. It was only slowly that people in the churches realised that human rights were also involved in God's concern with men and women. And the learning process certainly took its time. For after all the consciousness of human rights was already emerging in the thirteenth century. It was crystallising out even then, in language and in law. The *Magna Charta* of 1215 is witness, as well as all the documents that followed it.

3.3. Admittedly, the cause of human rights was not as obvious in past eras as it is today, and its infringement did not take the same form. Information about the disregard of human rights was not so quickly and clearly available all over the world as is the case today—if only because of the methods of communication that did not exist earlier as they do today. Perhaps even the extent and the negative quality of the violations have grown disproportionately, because people have acquired a tremendous increase of power over people, by means of secret police and through new instruments of a military, economic and technical-adminstrative kind. To this is added the danger of the manipulation of human life through medicine or technical development. Because they are ahead in technology or power, thoughtless nations or conscienceless systems of power can make the earth an uninhabitable planet for other countries—and indeed for the whole of mankind. Earlier, environmental protection as a human right hardly existed. Whereas former eras had primarily to fight against nature and natural forces in order to secure survival, man's existence is probably threatened most, taking history as a whole, from the side of life to which he at the same time owes his progress: human society. The temptation to misuse society's power is (perhaps) greater today than it was earlier. The storm warnings are clearer than ever before. Never was it more urgent to use the regulating systems of law and morals to steer social behaviour on to a plane where it is binding for the whole of mankind, so as to protect from misuse the liberties that have been developed. This is probably one of the reasons why a sense of the importance of human rights has increased to such a degree.

3.4. *In this context the Churches are offered a social task of pre-eminent importance*: to promote the consciousness of human rights and the respect for them, i.e., *to promote an appropriate sense of human rights in co-operative solidarity.* Here what is at issue is not least a moral educative goal and a moral education; and it is towards this that the churches' social work in family, congregation, school and other sectors of public life would have to be directed.

Certainly, the importance of human rights on the level of national or international law must not be diminished. That human rights should have grown beyond the framework of civil rights in individual countries is one of the great progressive steps in the growth of law. State sovereignty and the claim to non-intervention in 'internal affairs' no longer has unlimited validity—for example where human rights are disregarded by states which signed the Helsinki agreement, or the United Nations covenants on human rights in 1966. These states can now be pinned down by the legal obligations they have taken on themselves. But we must not deceive ourselves. The instrument of law has only very limited opportunities of influencing social reality. Numerous spheres of public and private behaviour are beyond the arm of the law. Only extreme cases of the law's violation are actionable. A considerable number of positive claims (the right to work, the right to education, the right to co-determination or workers' participation, and so on) are to a large extent not actionable at all.

Where a development of the sense of responsibility for human rights is lacking, positive law can do very little. Even the hope that apparently still inspired Ernst Topitsch[16] has proved partly vain; for he hoped that human rights would leave behind them natural law's susceptibility to ideology and would escape from their openness to manipulation, by virtue of their logical clarity and their specific distinctness of directive. The developments of recent decades have shown that *a sense of humanity—which means a morally binding respect for people—is of imperative importance.* It should be a special task for the Churches to develop the moral consciousness in the interests of human rights and to evolve patterns of behaviour which may help to realise human rights on the basis of freely accepted and freely affirmed moral claims; and this task should cover both the development of theory, and practice among people.

3.5. Here the Churches must see it as a moral duty to work off their own deficit in the matter of human rights, a deficit to which I have already several times drawn attention. For Catholicism, the Synod of Bishops expressed a demand of this kind quite unequivocally in 1971. The Church, it said, must first of all put into practice itself, in its own behaviour and its own life, what it demands of society outside the Church.[17] 'In the Church's own sphere, every right is to be observed without reserve or condition. No one, whatever his relations to the Church may be, should have the rights that belong to everyone curtailed.'[18] I suppose it is hardly necessary to prove that the Church's practice is still far from fulfilling this postulate. Equally, considerable theoretical work must be carried out in order to expose the pseudo-legitimation of those attitudes and institutions in the Church which date from the period when it disapproved of human rights.

There would seem to be an urgent need here *to take stock of the rights that have been infringed, through an empirical investigation of ecclesiastical practice,* by enquiring into the law as it really exists and behaviour as it actually is. I have already given earlier, in another place,[19] a few examples of infringements of the right to marriage and a family, and contraventions of personal rights and liberties: for example, an accused person's right to a hearing; or the right to have freedom of opinion and liberty of conscience respected, in the Church as well. Johannes Neumann has explored this complex of problems in more detail.[20] We can pick out particular examples again and again from the Church's daily press. Here a sacristan is dismissed from the Church's service because, after the death of his wife, he marries again, for his own sake and the sake of his numerous children—and his second wife's divorce is not valid according to canon law. There a theology professor loses his livelihood because, as a priest who has reverted to lay status, he marries. In another case a woman doctor is dismissed from a Catholic hospital because she has felt obliged to leave her Church for reasons of conscience.

Admittedly all this is controversial material. But are the controversies to be solved by the simple rebuke that here we have to do with 'the internal affairs' of the Catholic Church? And that the Catholic Church is quite simply a community with a certain purpose and accordingly has the right to enforce discipline within itself? What has the Church to observe first and pre-eminently: the rights of every person, rights which he possesses *as* person, or the law promulgated by the Church itself, which serves the preservation and development of its own system? *Here the Church is faced with tasks similar to those of sovereign states, whose particular claims to sovereignty must allow themselves to be questioned—and if necessary restricted—by the general, that is to say the all-embracing, justice which forms the basis of human rights.* The primary character of human rights must be recognised by the Church as well, and recognised in a double sense: on the one hand, inasmuch as the ethical content of human rights goes before even the legal enactments of the Church and takes precedence over them; and on the other, in so far as human rights, as morally effective motivating forces or *idée force,* have continually to act as a challenge to the affirmation and establishment of greater justice, in the sense of human rights.

3.6. Here the Church is faced with immense tasks of internal reform. But if it fails to carry out that reform, it cannot adequately fulfil its task for society. In view of research into the personality, it is impossible to deny the mutual influence of social environment (as social system) and the formation of character.[21] The Church will not be able to form characters that are open to, and conscious of, human rights if through its social influence and on the basis of its own structure it produces patterns of thinking and behaviour that are in contradiction to the rights of personality and the right to liberty; or if it develops an attitude of privilege in the people belonging to its own system, and a defence mechanism towards 'people of different beliefs' contrary to human rights.

Admittedly, the Church is faced with particular difficulties here. For, as a community of people of like beliefs and similar purposes, it is bound to be intent on preserving and developing its notions of value and its ideas about life. It is bound to seek for adherents and a community which will build up a sense of belonging together—and which by that very fact will cut itself off from 'outsiders'. Moreover all this happens in most religious systems, at least in Christianity, for it springs from the interpretation of this faith as being the only true religion. Consequently practising members of the Church especially are all too easily susceptible to intolerant patterns of thinking and behaviour.

It would be difficult to show that a sense of tolerance, or the practice of tolerance, developed to an exemplary degree in Christian history. But a peaceful living-together of nations, races and cultures, of political systems and religions, is not possible without *the continually new practice and development of constructive tolerance.* Without this human rights are inconceivable. We may term true tolerance *the* cardinal virtue for the social ethics of our time. We still have to achieve its conceptually more precise definition, as well as the anchoring of human rights in the doctrinal system of a theologically based social ethic. But above all tolerance must be made present reality by the Church, as a group with experience in the realm of moral behaviour. Training in tolerance must become a central task for the Church's moral education, and must be directly linked with the communication of its meaning in the light of faith.

3.7. For here *the specific opportunity of Christian ethics in the cause of human rights* really becomes evident. Its theological premiss makes this ethic an incomparable basis for unprejudiced solidarity with everyone, simply as person. Where we are ruled by the belief that God has accepted every one of us without any pre-conditions, and that he therefore makes his bestowal of himself dependent neither on proper human behaviour, nor on adherence to any religious, political or cultural system, or to any particular race or class—then man must be respected and affirmed, simply as man. We know that the New Testament actually uses the word love for this turning of God's towards us. Nor does the New Testament leave us in any doubt that—in spite of all our experience of the violation of human rights—the realisation of a new humanity is not impossible.

Translated by Margaret Kohl

Notes

1. 'Criticism of religion ends with the doctrine that man is for man the highest of beings, i.e., with the categorical imperative to overthrow all conditions in which man is a humilitated, enslaved, forsaken and despised being': Karl Marx *Einleitung zur 'Kritik der Hegelschen Rechtsphilosophie'* (1844) quoted in Ernst Bloch *Das Prinzip Hoffnung* (Frankfurt 1959) p. 1607.
2. Hans Albert 'Ethik und Meta-Ethik. Das Dilemma der analytischen Moral-philosophie' *Archiv für Philosophie* 11 (1961) pp.28-63; reprinted in *Werturteilsstreit* ed. Hans Albert and Ernst Topitsch (Darmstadt 1971) pp. 472-517.
3. Stephan H. Pfürtner 'Ökumene als Chance und Herausforderung zu freier Menschlichkeit' *Ökum. Rundschau* 23 (1974) pp. 139-154, esp. here pp. 147 ff.
4. Cf. Wolfgang Huber 'Zur theologischen Interpretation und zur gegenwärtigen kirchlichen Bedeutung der Menschenrechte' *Diakonie. Zeitschrift des Diakonischen Werkes der Evang. Kirche Deutschlands,* 4. Jahrgang (1977) Heft 3, pp. 144-147, here esp. p. 144.
5. E.g., *ibid* No. 34 ff.
6. See also S. H. Pfürtner 'Die Menschenrechte in der römisch-katholischen Kirche' *Zeitschrift für Evang. Ethik* 20. Jahrgang (1976), Heft 1, pp. 35-63, esp. here pp. 40 ff.
7. John XXIII, Encyclical *Pacem in terris* (1963), No. 143.

8. *Ibid,* heading to No. 142 ff.

9. See Wolfgang Huber and Heinz Edward Tödt, *Menschenrechte. Perspecktiven einer menschlichen Welt* (Stuttgart, Berlin 1977) pp. 45 ff.

10. See for example the New Year's address given by Paul VI in 1969. It was under the heading of 'the promotion of human rights: a way to peace'. Paul VI, on the celebration of 'Peace Day' on Jan. 1, 1969, *Typis Polyglottis Vaticanis* (Rome 1968) p. 11.

11. W. Huber and H. E. Tödt, *op. cit.,* pp. 55 ff (see n.9).

12. Helmut Thieliecke, *Theologische Ethik,* vol. II, Pt. 2: *Ethik des Politischen* (Tübingen 1958; ET and abridgement, *Theological Ethics* (Philadelphia 1966)). In the various sections Thieliecke talks about human rights in only 42 paragraphs out of a total of 4,381. At the same time they are one of his express themes, even though they occupy no central place in his systematic outline.

13. Walter Kreck *Grundfragen christlicher Ethik* (Munich 1975). Kreck does not expressly devote any particular section to human rights. They do crop up, not least in the context of other terms (the same, incidentally, may be said of Thieliecke, cf. n. 12), but they are by no means one of the points emphasised in his scheme.

14. Heinz-Horst Schrey *Einführung in die evangelische Soziallehre* (Darmstadt 1973) pp. 86, 98, 105; but Schrey only points to the isolated discussion of human rights.

15. W. Huber and H. E. Tödt, *op. cit.,* p. 45 (see n. 9).

16. Ernst Topitsch, *Die Menschenrechte als Problem der Ideologiekritik* and *Sozialphilosophie zwischen Ideologie und Wissenschaft* (Neuwied, Berlin 1966) pp. 71-97.

17. *De justitia in mundo* ('Justice in the World'), declaration of the Synod of Bishops, 1971, No. 41. Printed in *Texte zur katholischen Soziallehre* (Kevelaer 1976) pp. 525-548, esp. p. 537.

18. *Ibid.* No. 42.

19. S. H. Pfürtner *op. cit.,* pp. 54-62 (see n. 6) and *Macht, Recht, Gewissen in Kirche und Gesellschaft* (Zürich, Einsiedeln, Cologne 1972) pp. 29-52 and 224-273.

20. Johannes Neumann *Menschenrechte—auch in der Kirche?* (Zürich, Einsiedeln, Cologne 1976).

21. See for example Theodor W. Adorno *Studien zum autoritären Charakter* (Frankfurt 1973).

James A. Coriden

Human Rights in the Church: A Matter of Credibility and Authenticity

1. THE WORDS

SOME SCHOLARS have attempted to demonstrate that the Church has proclaimed what we now refer to as 'human rights' from its very beginning. Mainly they find the teaching on rights implicit in certain theological themes, e.g., man's creation in the image of God, Christ's mandate of love of neighbour and His salvific death for all people, human dignity based on the indwelling of the spirit, freedom as a characteristic of the Kingdom, etc.[1] Whether or not this case for long historical roots is convincing, there can be little doubt about the Church's insistent preaching on human rights since the time of Pope Leo XIII's celebrated encyclical on the rights of workers (*Rerum Novarum* 1891). The proclamation has become more intense, frequent and detailed in the past two decades, especially since John XXIII's letter on Christianity and social progress (*Mater et Magistra* 1961), the Second Vatican Council's Pastoral Constitution on the Church in the Modern World, (*Gaudium et Spes* 1965), and Paul VI's encyclical on the development of peoples (*Populorum Progressio* 1967). The teaching is earnest and genuine, but is it believable? In part, the credibility of the message rests on the performance of the witness. Does the Church do as it says others should do in respect to human rights? This question will be the chief concern of this article. Its purview is limited largely to the Roman Catholic Church in North America.

If there was any lingering doubt about the legitimacy of the Church's involvement in the area of human rights or about its place on the Church's agenda, the statements of two recent international Synods of Bishops surely dispelled it: 'Action on behalf of justice and participation in the transformation of the world appear to us as a constitutive dimension of the preaching of the Gospel, or, in other words, of the Church's mission for the redemption of the human race and its liberation from every oppressive situation.'[2] J. Bryan Hehir, a foremost spokesman for the American Church on matters of justice and peace, in commenting on this statement, accurately assessed its import: 'The theological and pastoral significance of this passage cannot be underestimated. Briefly, it means that work for justice is essential to the Church, pertaining to its innermost nature and mission.'[3]

In their 1974 Synod on evangelisation the bishops affirmed 'their determination to promote human rights and reconciliation everywhere, in the Church and in the contemporary world'. They stated that the Church 'firmly . . . believes that the promotion of human rights is a requirement of the Gospel and as such must occupy a central position in its ministry'. They specified certain rights which are more directly menaced today such as the right to live, to have enough to eat, the right to religious liberty, social and economic rights, and political and cultural rights.[4] These recent high-level statements reassert and deepen the involvement of the Church in the field of human rights which has been proclaimed by Popes and an ecumenical council.

This principle follows upon that involvement: witness to human rights is credible and effective only when it is not contradicted by internal counter-witness by which the Church denies those same rights to its members or those who come in contact with it. In other words, a respect for human rights must find an authentic resonance in the inner life and activity of the Church. This principle has been recognised and affirmed by the two successive Episcopal Synods cited above: 'While the Church is bound to give witness to justice, she recognises that anyone who ventures to speak to people about justice must first be just in their eyes.'[5] 'From her own experience the Church knows that her ministry of fostering human rights in the world requires continued scrutiny and purification of her own life, her laws, institutions and policies. . . . In the Church, as in other institutions and groups, purification is needed in internal practices and procedures, and in relationships with social structures and systems whose violations of human rights deserve censure.[6]

The principle was sharpened and made more explicit by the Pontifical Commission on Justice and Peace in a valuable working paper, 'The Church and Human Rights' (issued December 10, 1974): 'If her evangelical mission is to be effective, the Church must first and foremost stimulate in the world the recognition, observance, protection and promotion of the rights of the human person, beginning with an act of self-examination, a hard look at the manner and degree in which fundamental rights are observed and applied within her own organisation.' (No. 62)

2. THE FACTS

For the purposes of analysis, it is possible to consider three groups of people whom the Church encounters and whose rights it influences:

(1) Non-Catholics: those other Christians, members of other faiths, or 'unchurched' persons who come in contact with the Church;
(2) Members of the Church: the baptised and those in the catechumenate;
(3) Priests and others in the full-time employ of the Church.

(1) The areas of evangelisation and ecumenism afford examples of improved treatment and increased respect for the rights of others on the part of the Church. In its missionary efforts since the Second Vatican Council the Church has focused far more on Christian service and witness and far less on aggressive proselytisation. This resulted from a heightened appreciation for religious freedom (based on human dignity and the essential freedom of the act of faith) and for the effective saving power of God outside the Church.[7] The effect of this change in policy has been to render the Church in mission areas (both foreign and domestic) a more benign and less threatening presence; it shows a greater respect for the rights and freedom of those whom it contacts.

Similarly in formal religious relationships with non-Catholics, since it joined the ecumenical movement, the Church had become less arrogant and overbearing. For example, mitigated 'promises' in mixed marriages regarding the rearing of children, dispensations from the 'canonical form' permitting such marriages to take place in non-Catholic churches, abolition of the excommunication for marriages before non-Catholic ministers,[8] enabling the burial of non-Catholics in Catholic cemeteries, fostering joint worship, co-operation, and (exceptionally) even sacramental sharing in the interests of Christian unity[9]—all these ecumenically-prompted legal changes are significant gestures of amity and show a genuinely higher regard for the consciences and religious liberty of non-Catholics.

On the other hand, there is still some way to go. The retention of the mandatory canonical form (i.e., Catholics must be married before a deputed priest and two witnesses) and the necessary assurance by the Catholic party that he/she will do everything possible to rear the children in the Catholic faith are ecumenically offensive and indicate a less than full regard for the religious freedom of those who are not members of the Church.[10]

(2) Toward the rights of its own members the Church has shown a much greater sensitivity in recent years, but there remain serious shortcomings. The principal advance is also the area of chief deficiency: effective, active participation of the laity in responsible decision-making in the life of the Church. After the Council there were important steps taken toward the inclusion of lay persons in significant roles of responsibility. Parish councils and diocesan pastoral councils were formed, and lay people were included in diocesan synods and many other important advisory bodies. Efforts to promote co-responsibility for all members of the Church were serious and widespread.[11] Unfortunately an overall assessment of the success of these efforts at this point must result in a negative judgment. For many reasons the attempts of laity to become equally responsible partners in the direction of the Church have borne fruit which is more symbolic than real—effective power has not left the hands of the clergy.[12] This inability to exercise any real voice or vote in their own religious community is a partial denial of the human right to self-determination. The failure in co-responsibility or participation has many facets, e.g., full and candid financial disclosure, voice in the selection of pastors and bishops, sharing in allocation of resources, and review of programmes and policies.[13]

Closely related to this deficient participation, and even more sharply discriminatory, is the exclusion of women from ordained ministry coupled with the exclusive access to all effective authority by the ordained clergy. It is a near-perfect design for the retention of a male power elite in a Church which is at least half female.

(3) Priests and other full-time employees of the Church have the greatest influence and advantage in the community of faith, but, since they are uniquely dependent on the Church, and consequently vulnerable, their rights most need protection. Here again very significant advances have been made in the past fifteen years, for example, salaries have increased, retirement and medical and other 'fringe' benefits have improved, priests have formed senates or councils which are concerned about their welfare, personnel boards, assignment policies and grievance procedures have been inaugurated in many places, and collective bargaining for lay teachers and hospital employees has been accepted in some places.

However, in spite of these important gains in areas of human rights, much remains to be done. Very often the new policies, procedures and boards are empty and ineffective in practice. They are more illusory than real, a form of 'window-dressing'.

(*a*) Priests' senates have proven ineffectual for the most part; they have secured certain benefits for the clergy, but they do not share power or decision-making in a significant way.[14]

(*b*) Personnel assignments and transfers are still done in a remote and arbitrary way in most places, with little opportunity for real consultation.

(*c*) Teachers and other employees are sometimes dismissed because of admitted homosexual orientation or attempted re-marriage after divorce.

(*d*) Grievance procedures or mechanisms to settle disputes are rarely available or effective; sometimes their results are ignored or overruled.

(*e*) Organising for collective bargaining on the part of lay employees has been stoutly and vigorously resisted in some places, even though the right to organise is amost a first principle of Catholic social doctrine.

(*f*) Retirement benefits and medical care for lay employees is either non-existent or woefully inadequate in some Church-related institutions.

(*g*) Finally, a fundamental human right, the right to marry, is still denied to bishops, priests and deacons despite the fact that convincing arguments for the universal, mandatory retention of celibacy have not been forthcoming.

3. THE STEPS TO IMPROVEMENT

These few examples illustrate that the Church has serious deficiencies in several areas of human rights—affecting non-members, members, and employees. It is at least arguable that these shortcomings inhibit its witness to and proclamation of human rights to the world. How can this 'credibility gap' be bridged? More profoundly, how can the Church's inner life and operation be brought into an authentic correspondence with its teaching on social justice and the rights of the human person? There are no easy answers to these questions, and no single programme will guarantee that everyone's rights will always be respected by the Church. But there are at least two important steps which can and should be taken in order to bring the inner life of the Church into greater harmony with its teachings on social justice and human rights:

(1) Issue a clear declaration of the rights of Church members;
(2) Establish effective processes for the vindication of the stated rights.

(1) A statement or bill of rights, if it represents a real consensus of convictions, does two things: it commits the community to certain stated standards of respect for the dignity of persons, and it gives individuals both a consciousness of their own rights and a sense of how they should

treat one another. In addition, if the declaration of rights is included in a constitution or promulgated as law, it provides solid grounds for the protection of personal and communal rights.

Several attempts have been made to articulate such a declaration of rights for the Church—with varying degrees of success. This is one based on authoritative documents:

> In accordance with the authentic teaching of the Catholic Church, the members of this Canon Law Society of America express their conviction that all persons in the Church are fundamentally equal in regard to their common rights and freedoms, among which are:
>
> The right to freedom to hear the Word of God and to participate in the sacramental and liturgical life of the Church;
>
> The right and freedom to exercise the apostolate and share in the mission of the Church;
>
> The right and freedom to speak and be heard and to receive objective information regarding the pastoral needs and affairs of the Church;
>
> The right to education, to freedom of inquiry and to freedom of expression in the sacred sciences;
>
> The right to free assembly and association in the Church; and such inviolable and universal rights of the human person as the right to the protection of one's reputation, to respect of one's person, to activity in accord with the upright norm of one's conscience, to protection of privacy.
>
> The dignity of the human person, the principles of fundamental fairness, and the universally applicable presumption of freedom require that no member of the Church arbitrarily be deprived of the exercise of any right or office.[15]

The 1971 Synod document 'Justice in the World' contains an attenuated list of rights related to social justice.[16] More recently a group of French theologians signed and published a '*Manifeste de la Liberté* Chrétienne' consisting of fifteen broadly stated rights and hopes.[17] The proposed draft of the 'Fundamental Law of the Church', prepared by the Commission for Revision of the Code of Canon Law, contains a section entitled 'The Fundamental Rights and Obligations of All the Faithful' (canons 10-25). These canons basically express: (*a*) the equality of the faithful, (*b*) the right to share in the mission of the Church, (*c*) the rights of inquiry, expression, and association, (*d*) the right to participate in the government of the Church, and, (*e*) procedural and remedial rights. However, these rights are set forth in a form that is both vague and limiting, heavily conditioned in their very expression. Canon 19 serves as a final qualifier: 'In the use of their rights, it is fitting that the faithful observe the principle of personal and social responsibility: in exercising their rights both as individuals and as members of associations, they must keep in mind the common good of the Church and also the rights of other people and their own obligations toward others; it is the responsibility of ecclesiastical authority in the light of the common good, to control the exercise of the rights which are proper to the faithful or even to restrict them by invalidating and incapacitating laws.[18] This formulation seems quite inadequate and has been widely criticised.[19]

A more positive and sweeping affirmation of 'Christian Rights' emerged from a symposium on a 'Declaration of Christian Freedoms' held at Catholic University (Washington) in 1968:

1. The right to freedom in the search for truth, without fear of administrative sanctions.
2. The right to freedom in expressing personal beliefs and opinions as they appear to the individual, including freedom of communication and publication.
3. The right of individuals to access to objective information, in particular about the internal and external operations of the Church.
4. The right to develop the unique potentialities and personality traits proper to the individual without fear of repression by the Christian community or Church authorities.
5. The right of the Christian to work out his salvation in response to the unique challenges offered by the age and society in which he lives.
6. The rights of persons employed by, or engaged in the service of, the Church to conditions of work consonant with human dignity as well as their right to professional practices comparable to those in the society at large.
7. All members of the Church have the right to freedom of assembly and of association.
8. All members of the Church have the right to participate, according to their gift from the Spirit, in the teaching, government, and sanctification of the Church.
9. All members of the Church are entitled to all the rights and freedoms of Christians without discrimination on the basis of race, colour, sex, birth, language, political opinion, or national or social origin.
10. All members of the Church have a right to effective remedies for the redress of grievances and the vindication of their rights.
11. In all proceedings in which one of the parties may suffer substantial disadvantage, the procedure must be fair and impartial, with an opportunity for submission to boards of mediation and arbitration.
12. In all procedures, administrative or judicial, in which penalties may be imposed, the accused shall not be deprived of any right, office or

communion with the Church except by due process of law; said due process shall include, but not be limited to, the right not to be a witness against oneself; the right to a speedy and public trial; the right to be informed in advance of the specific charge against him; the right to confront the witnesses against him; the right to have the assistance of experts and of counsel for his defense; and a right of appeal.[20]

(2) Effective and realistic procedures for the vindication of rights are even more important than the declaration of those rights. Without respected and available mechanisms to settle disputes and redress grievances, the best 'bill of rights' can be rendered meaningless. The establishment of good processes for 'doing justice and equity' is an absolutely critical need—in the Church as elsewhere.

The Commission for the Revision of the Code acknowledged this need and the Episcopal Synod of 1967 agreed when the Synod approved a series of 'Principles to Direct the Revision of the Code' proposed by the Commission. Among them: 'The rights of each one of the faithful must be recognised and protected . . . the principle of juridical protection must be proclaimed in canon law and applied equally to superiors and subjects so that all suspicion of arbitrariness in ecclesiastical administration is entirely eliminated.' They acknowledged that recourse against administrative decisions is lacking in the Church. 'Hence there is felt a need to set up a series of administrative tribunals in the Church, and to evolve proper canonical procedures at each level for the defense of rights.'[21]

An adequate system of *fora* for the defense of personal or communal rights still does not exist in the Church, but some have been created in many dioceses and others are being proposed. In 1969 the National Conference of Catholic Bishops received and endorsed a report 'On Due Process' from a committee of the Canon Law Society of America. It recommended excellent procedures for conciliation (mediated dialogue) and arbitration (voluntary reference to an impartial person) of controversies as well as structures for administrative decision-making (to forestall disputes).[22] Many dioceses and religious communities subsequently established 'due process' boards or grievance procedures, and in some instances they have functioned effectively. In most places, however, they either do not exist or they are not used or their decisions are ignored. The need remains for local, accessible, and relatively uncomplicated structures to settle disputes and vindicate rights.

The Commission for Revision of the Code has proposed a system of administrative tribunals which holds considerable promise.[23] It calls for a series of less formal courts—at diocesan, regional and national levels—for recourse against administrative decisions which are seen to be inequitable or injurious to rights. Even though there are some defects in the proposal, it will be a refreshing and hopeful innovation in the Church's legal structure, if and when it is promulgated. The tribunals and other procedures will only be successful, obviously, if they are in fact set up everywhere, adequately staffed, encouraged to function, and if they gain people's respect for actually doing justice.

'Anyone who ventures to speak to people about justice must first be just in their eyes.'[24] The Church must show respect for the rights of persons if it is to be a credible witness to those rights in the world. 'The Church is called to engage in continuing self-examination in order to make its own structures and procedures more effective instuments of an witness to . . . divine justice.'[25] But there is an even more profound reason why the Church must be ardently solicitous for human rights in its own life and activities: to be true to itself and its mission.

Notes

1. Confer A. Miller (ed.) *A Christian Declaration on Human Rights* (Theological Studies of the World Alliance of Reformed Churches), (Grand Rapids 1977); J. Haughey (ed.) *The Faith That Does Justice: Examining the Christian Sources for Social Change* (New York 1977); A. Falconer 'The Churches and Human Rights' in *One in Christ* 13:4 (1977) pp. 321-50; E. Saunders 'The Bible and Human Rights', a paper for the National Council of Churches Commission on Faith and Order Seminar on Human Rights, March 1978.
2. *Justice in the World* Statement of 1971 Synod, Introduction. Eng. trans., (Washington: N.C.C.B., 1971) p. 34.
3. Why Is The Church Involved? *Human Rights, Human Needs—An Unfinished Agenda* (Washington: U.S.C.C., 1978) p. 19.
4. *Human Rights and Reconciliation* Statement issued by the 1974 Synod 'Origins' 4:20 (1974) p. 318-9. A more complete enumeration of rights appears in *Gaudium et Spes,* nos. 26-9, and the Working Paper of the Pontifical Commission on Justice and Peace *The Church and Human Rights* (Vatican City 1975) nos. 36-9, contains a full list.
5. *Justice in the World, op. cit.,* p. 44.
6. *Human Rights and Reconciliation, op. cit.,* p. 319. A similar concern was expressed ecumenically in the Report of the Baden Consultation on Christian Concern for Peace *Peace, The Desperate Imperative* (Geneva: S.O.D.E.P.A.X., 1970) no. 86.
7. *Lumen Gentium,* 15-17; *Dignitatis Humanae,* 2-4, 9-10; *Ad Gentes,* 11-12.
8. *Matrimonia Mixta* Cong. for Doctrine of Faith, 31st March 1970.
9. *Ecumenical Directory* Secretariat for Christian Unity, 14th May 1967.

10. Confer the *Final Report of the Anglican-Roman Catholic Commission on Theology of Marriages and Its Application to Mixed Marriages* 27th June 1975, (Washington: U.S.C.C., 1976) nos. 56-72.

11. For example *Who Decides for the Church? Studies in Co-Responsibility* J. Coriden (ed.), (Hartford: C.L.S.A., 1971) also published as *Jurist* 31:1, (1971).

12. R. Schoenher & E. Simpson 'Comparative Religious Organisation Study' University of Wisconsin, as reported in the *National Catholic Reporter* 14:36 (28th July, 1978) pp. 1 and 4.

13. These issues and many others were forthrightly raised in 'A Call to Action' Conference, Detroit, Oct., 1976 (published in *Origins* 6:20 and 21, 1976 pp. 309-40), and responded to in *To Do the Work of Justice: A Plan of Action for the Catholic Community in the United States* 4th May 1978 (Washington: U.S.C.C., 1978).

14. Schoenher and Simpson, *op. cit.,* p. 4.

15. *On Due Process,* A Summary of the Actions Taken by the N.C.C.B. on the Subject of Due Process, (Washington: N.C.C.B. 1969) p. 4-5.

16. *Op. cit.*, p. 44-5.

17. Dated Easter, 1975, and published in *Le Supplément* 125 (May 1978) pp. 301-9.

18. *Schema Legis Ecclesiae Fundamentalis,* Textus Emendatus, (Vatican 1971).

19. For example, by committees of the Canon Law Society of America *Jurist* 31 (1971) 342-62 and *American Ecclesiastical Review* 165 (1971) pp. 3-17.

20. Excerpted from a consensus paper 'Towards a Declaration of Christian Rights' in *The Case for Freedom: Human Rights in the Church* J. Coriden (ed.), (Washington: Corpus, 1969) pp. 5-14.

21. *Communicationes* 2 (1969) p. 82-3.

22. *Op. cit.,* pp. 13-34.

23. *Schema Canonum De Procedura Administrativa* (Vatican 1972). Revised, it now finds its place as canons 397-435 in the *Schema Canonum De Modo Procedendi Pro Tutela Iurium Seu De Processibus* (Vatican 1976). For a description and evaluation, confer R. Kennedy 'Administrative Law: New Proposed Roman Norms' in *Canon Law Society of America Proceedings* (1972) pp. 98-103.

24. *Justice in the World, loc. cit.,* p. 44.

25. *To Do The Work of Justice, loc. cit.,* p. 23.

PART III

The Praxis

François Refoulé

Efforts made on behalf of Human Rights by the Supreme Authority of the Church

1. PAUL VI

'DEFENDER of human dignity, herald of the rights of man and of the ending of all social discrimination, upholder of religious liberties, champion of peace in the world': it was in these words that the ecumenical patriarch Dimitrios referred to Pope Paul VI the day after he died. These words are, in fact, very apt. There can be no pope in history—with the possible exception of John XXIII during his brief pontificate—who 'took man's side' so indefatigably and so tenaciously. Anyone who takes the trouble to glance through the late pope's output—encyclicals, addresses to the diplomatic corps, letters to secretaries-general of the UNO or to various international agencies, messages to the world, homilies etc.—cannot but be impressed by the place occupied by the defence of the dignity and rights of man.[1] And the words he spoke at the UNO in 1965 are unforgettable: 'We make our own the voice of the poor, the disinherited, the wretched, those who long for justice, a dignified life, freedom, well-being and progress'. The same goes for the letter he wrote to Kurt Waldheim, Secretary-general of the UNO in 1972: 'The Church feels wounded in her own person whenever a man's rights are disregarded or violated, whoever he is and whatever it is about'. And so too with the last words of his message to the whole world in 1974 at the end of the Synod of Bishops: 'We declare our determination to promote the rights of man and reconciliation amongst men, in the Church and in the world today'. Equally well known is his concern to ensure the representation of the Holy See in all international organisations, which is why he welcomed the invitation to attend the conferences of Helsinki and Belgrade. By the same token it was he who chose the theme of 'Justice in the World' for the Synod of Bishops in 1971, just as it was he who had created the commission *Justice and Peace* in 1967, one of the aims of which is 'to contribute to a deeper study of the problems of development and peace, especially in their doctrinal, pastoral and apostolic aspect'.

What it is important to note in all this is that Paul VI never failed to refer explicitly to the Universal Declaration of the Rights of Man in all the efforts he made to promote and defend the rights of man. He wanted to make it the corner-stone of all his work, and that is why he always commended it. In 1968 he referred to it as 'the path that must not be abandoned if mankind today sincerely wants to consolidate peace'; in 1970 he called it, with reference to the UNO, 'one of its finest titles to glory'. In the same spirit, he never lost an opportunity not only of assuring it of his 'complete moral support for the common ideal contained in the Universal Declaration and for the greater and greater consolidation of the rights of man which are expressed therein', but also of expressing his confidence about the implementation of this ideal.

2. IN A LINE OF DESCENT

Granted the high priority Paul VI attached to the rights of man, is it not then surprising that he did not devote at least an apostolic letter, even if not an encyclical, to the subject? There is nothing strange about this attitude: in 'taking man's side' Paul VI simply thought of himself as following on where John XXIII and Vatican II had left off and he thought it was enough to refer to the encyclical *Pacem in terris* and to the documents of the Council, in particular *Gaudium et spes*. And it is in fact to John XXIII that belongs the credit of having made the defence and promotion of the rights of man one of the chief concerns of the Church's action in the world. It is, nevertheless true, as Cardinal Roy stressed in 1973, that '*Pacem in terris* was in a deep sense an inheritance before it became a heritage' and that is 'had received as much as it gave'. Without the courageous encyclicals of Pius XI against the totalitarianism of Hitler and atheistic communism, without the Christmas messages of Pius XII during the war years, and particularly those of 1941 and 1942 and that of 1944 on democracy, without the same pope's profound reflections on the state, economic and social affairs,[2] the encyclical *Pacem in terris* would be scarcely thinkable. There is a clear line of continuity between Pius XII and John XXIII. But drawing attention to John XXIII's debt to his immediate predecessors takes away nothing of the encyclical's originality or boldness. The measure of this is the position John XXIII takes up in regard to the Universal Declaration of the Rights of Man and of the UNO when compared with the corresponding attitude of Pius XII. For in the whole of the latter's nevertheless vast output, there is not the slightest reference to the Declaration of 1948. Why this astonishing silence? Pius XII never gave an explanation himself. My own view is that he criticised it for not basing the rights of man on the order established by God for mankind. His encyclical *Summi pontificatus* of 1939 shows that in his eyes society could be saved only by a public recognition of the law of Christ. He was no less vigorous in denouncing the 'futility of any merely human effort purporting to replace the law of Christ by anything else that equalled it'. He may also have been critical of its formal and individualistic character. Whatever the reason, *Pacem in terris* is in strong contrast with the silence of Pius XII and not only opens with a grand charter of the rights and duties of man, quite obviously inspired by the Universal Declaration, but approves of the latter, even though it also qualifies it somewhat. The charter of *Pacem in terris* is, however, no simple copy of the Declaration. John XXIII seeks to redress the imbalances of the latter, forcefully stressing man's social being and, in consequence, the reciprocity of rights and duties. The criticism of the Declaration that was implicit in *Pacem in terris* was, moreover, to be taken up and made more explicit by *Gaudium et spes.* Mgr. Haubtmann has disclosed that section 30 of the pastoral constitution, entitled *The need to go beyond an individualistic ethic,* was drafted at the request of a number of bishops concerned to alert Christians to the danger of individualism that ran through the Declaration of 1948 as much as that of 1789, even though the former added to the latter an acknowledgment of social rights and thereby presupposed social life, since social rights are necessarily 'the fruit of social life and solidarity'.[4] The existence of these reservations and criticisms makes it all the more remarkable that John XXIII and, in his wake, Vatican II and Paul VI should have approved of the Universal Declaration of 1948, hailing it not only 'as a step towards the establishment of a juridico-political organisation of the world community' but also as a meeting-place of Church and state. It is difficult to overestimate the importance of such an approbation.

This marks the close of the middle ages. What is more, the ideal of the moral society espoused by Leo XII and even by Pius XII in *Summi pontificatus* is also rejected as an anachronism. The papacy takes note both of the pluralism of contemporary societies and of the neutrality of the state. John XXIII nevertheless refuses to despair of the future of the world and has no intention of taking on the role of prophet of doom. He prefers to see in the universal aspiration of men towards greater justice, liberty and dignity expressed in the Declaration of 1948 not only a reason to hope but even the necessary basis for the construction of a society that is at once more humane and more in accord with the Gospel. This is a new way of looking at the world—as a place in the throes of travail. It was left to Paul VI and the Council to draw out all the implications of this.

The attitudes of John XXIII and Paul VI to the organisation of the United Nations also contrasts sharply with the more reserved and cautious attitude of Pius XII. It is true that the latter had prayed for its coming, especially in his famous Christmas message of 1944 on democracy; he had asked for it to be invested with real powers: 'The authority in such a society of the nations should be real and effective over all states forming its membership'. By the same token, he later, in his Christmas message of 1956, expressed the wish that the 'authority of the UNO be strengthened, especially for the purpose of securing general disarmanent'. It remains that he did not say much about it and that, when he did, it was to criticise its deficiencies. As early as 1946 he had already, in an allocution to the Sacred College at Christmas, asked what remained of the Charter of 1944, and answered himself: 'A shadow, a counterfeit'. His 1956 message expressed the same disenchantment. John XXIII and Paul VI, on the other hand, wished to place their confidence in the UNO. It is true that in *Pacem in terris* John XXIII followed the example of Pius XII in regretting the absence of a universal public authority capable of ensuring the effective guarantee of the rights proclaimed. He nevertheless expected a great deal from it. John XXIII and Paul VI were, therefore, perfectly well aware of the limitations and defects of the UNO but this did not stop them from thinking that it was the only possible partner in the task of constructing a juster and more inter-dependent society 'for man' today. As Pierre-Henri Simon had written earlier: 'Confusingly strident as it may be, the glass palace of Manhattan, illuminated at night, is a beacon of light to which the peoples of today's world look'.[6]

3. AN INNOVATOR

Heir to John XXIII as he may have been, and the man responsible for implementing the decisions of the Council as he was, Paul VI was, nevertheless, not just a 'copier'. He could not have been one, even if he had wanted to be. As Cardinal Roy felicitously put it when he was reflecting on *Pacem in terris* ten years after it had been promulgated, this encyclical remains an 'unfinished symphony'. To call it 'unfinished' is, of course, in no way to belittle it. It could not have been anything else. It emerged out of a particular political context, and nowadays history is gathering pace, so that the map of politics is different from what it was in 1963. It did, however, have certain undeniable weaknesses which Cardinal Roy had the honesty to point out, I shall here content myself with mentioning two of Paul VI's innovations, which are in any case partial. Had there been more space, I could also have noted his reflections on the particular historical conjuncture of the rights of man and on the conditions needed to translate the formal liberties proclaimed into realities. Here I can only advert to this.

(i) *The Status of Pronouncements by the Teaching Magisterium of the Church*

Even now it is worth rehearsing again the first words uttered by Paul VI to the UNO in 1965: 'Our meeting here . . . has two aspects: it is at once simple and grand. There is a simplicity about it because the man who is speaking to you is a man like yourselves; he is your brother, in fact one of the littlest in your company, since you represent sovereign states whereas he—if you care to look on us in this way—is invested with the tiniest and almost only symbolic temporal authority. . . . He has neither temporal power nor any ambition to compete with you. And the fact is that we have no demand to make, no question to put. The most we want to do is to express a wish, to ask for a favour, and that is the chance to offer you such service as we are competent to give, and that with disinterested humility and love'.

Every word is no doubt weighed and charged with meaning. These words carry the following implications:

(*a*) The recognition of the sovereignty of states. The Church today completely renounces the claim of the medieval Church to exercise power over the 'temporal city'; all it wishes to do is to 'offer its help', 'be of service to it'. Pius XII had already said as much in *Summi pontificatus.* Paul VI was to repeat it many times. The discourse to the UNO does, nevertheless, contain something new: Paul VI is not content to say that the Church wants to serve the world, what he says is: the Church want 'to be able to serve *you*'. He is offering an active collaboration with the UNO as well as with other international agencies. Paul VI was to say the same thing in January 1966 in his allocution to the diplomatic corps: 'So far as the Church is concerned, there is no ulterior motive in its desire to work with the powers of this world'.

(*b*) Recognition of the ideal proclaimed by the Declaration of 1948. Christians can share this ideal with all men of good will. This is why the Church is ready to support any efforts the UNO may make to promote the rights of man as much as it possibly can, without pretending 'to have an immediate solution to all the great questions pressing upon humanity' (*Gaudium et spes,* sections 33, 2), and without demanding a privileged position for itself. No, it will enter into dialogue with anyone. In other words, the Church acknowledges the leadership of the UNO in the defence and promotion of the rights of man, without thereby giving up the right to bring to bear a moral judgment on its activities, as the Synod of

Bishops was to recall in 1971. The seed of this double acknowledgment was no doubt contained in *Pacem in terris,* but it was Paul VI's achievement to have articulated this attitude more precisely.

(ii) *In the Name of the Gospel*

By what right and in what name is the teaching authority of the Church going to intervene in secular matters? Here Paul VI and Vatican II take up a somewhat different stance from that of John XXIII and *Pacem in terris.* This encyclical is, as we know, the first to have been addressed not only to Christians but also directly to 'all men of goodwill'. That is why in his desire to be understood by everybody John XXIII thought it only fitting to use the language of reason rather than of faith. The encyclical argues on the basis of a philosophy of natural law. According to Mgr. Haubtmann the first draft of the document of the Church in the modern world, *Gaudium et spes* (Schema 13, as it then was) used the same approach. This draft was turned down and the Council preferred to tackle the problem in another way. The constitution *Gaudium et spes* in its definitive form is constructed like an ascending spiral, starting at the bottom with very widely accepted truths and rising to the highest affirmations of faith. Throughout, however, Mgr. Haubtmann adds, 'and this must be underlined, the point of reference remains the Word of God, the Bible, and not any so-called natural order. . . . In other words, it is always the Church who speaks and it does so in its own key, which is the key of revelation. It is, to change the metaphor, this light of revelation which it projects on to all earthly realities'.[7] This way of tackling the problem is the one which Paul VI had elaborated in some detail in *Ecclesiam suam* (1964); it is the way of *dialogue.* Now it is most important that in a friendly dialogue each one says what he has to say and especially what it is specifically his to contribute. Paul VI recurs to this point in *Populorum progressio*: 'Sharing men's finest aspirations and suffering to see them unrealised, the Church wants to help them to find their complete fulfilment, and that is why it offers them what it is typically hers to offer: an integral vision of man and of mankind' (section 13). This is where the Church's specific contribution lies. 'Everybody may agree about building a new society which will be at the service of man', observes Paul VI in *Octogesima adveniens,* 'but we still have to know what sort of man we are talking about'. Now the Church is convinced that revelation sheds a master-light on man and on his dignity.

4. PAUL VI'S ACTIVITY AND ITS FRUIT

The ways in which the pope and indeed the Vatican as a whole act for the promotion and defence of the rights of man can, of course, be very diverse. The document of the Justice and Peace Commission mentions not only diplomatic action but making Christians and people in general aware and making prophetic denunciations. It is quite obvious that Paul VI himself preferred diplomatic activity (in a large sense of that word) and the education of Christians, and that is why, for example, he travelled to the UNO, to Asia, to Bogota. It is, of course, true that he also often denounced the violation of the rights of man and the social conditions which caused injustice. His discourses at Bogota and Medellin come to mind. But, except in the very rarest cases, his denunciations of the violation of human rights was limited to generalities. Some people, especially in Latin America, criticised him for this. Paul VI was aware of such criticism, but he never sought to justify his policy. His major preoccupations are, however, discernible.

In his apostolic letter *Octogesima adveniens* Paul VI himself underlines the fact that 'situations vary so much that we find it as difficult to say just the one right thing as to offer a solution of universal validity. . . . It is the business of particular Christian communities to analyse the situation of their own country as objectively as possible, to discern the issues and to take the measures that are appropriate . . .' (section 4). In this letter he addresses himself in the first place to layfolk, but he has something else in mind. Paul VI wanted to respect the prerogatives of the national conferences of bishops. It is their business to decide about the opportuneness of such and such an intervention or denunciation. And it is well known that the bishops of Latin America have in fact fully taken on these responsibilities. It is pretty remarkable that Paul VI never failed to support and encourage them.

We need, however, to press our reflections further. The art of political ethics, Père Valadier assures us, consists not in fixing upon some principle deemed to be determinative but in 'gaining a sense of the political totality and of the activities it requires in any given context. . . . The danger is that principle takes the place of practising the art of politics and that the brute facts of political life quickly boomerang on the idealist forced to act contrary to his will'.[10] This was also the gist of the reflections expressed in 1977 by Mgr. Casaroli, who was something in the nature of a minister of foreign affairs to Paul VI: 'A public condemnation is by no means always the best way of attaining one's desired aim. . . . What the authorities must do is to weigh the problems very carefully with realism but also with a deep respect for the demands of moral conscience.' He also intimated that the authorities sometimes found themselves faced by agonising and dramatic choices and asked those who did not hold such positions of responsibility and who did not always know all the facts not to criticise the authorities too readily.[11]

We should also add that Paul VI never stopped putting Christians on their guard against the temptation to violence. He no doubt did not want to say anything that could be construed as justifying violence.

So far as the fruits of the political activity of the Holy See since 1963 is concerned, it is difficult to measure the results, especially as Paul VI never intended to do more than support the efforts of the UNO and of the other international agencies and never sought to attribute anything to himself. What is clear is that apart from some progress, which is any case precarious enough, the results are in one sense disappointing. This is what explains the occasionally pessimistic tone of the discourses of Paul VI during his last years. At the same time, as Mgr. Silvestrini affirmed at the Belgrade conference, we have not got the right to despair: the movement in favour of basic freedoms has been given a decisive impetus and this movement is from now irreversible. 'A new conscience has been born', it has been said.[12] Is there any doubt that the Church has made a contribution to this event?

Translated by John Maxwell

Notes

1. See, for example, P.-E. Bolté *Les droits de l'homme et la papauté contemporaine* (Montreal 1975); Paul VI *Prendre parti pour l'homme* (Textes réunis et présentés par G. Defois) (Paris 1977); Pontifical commission Justitia et Pax *Document de travail No. 1, L'Eglise et les droits de l'homme* (Vatican 1975).

2. For the teaching of Pius XII, see J.-Y. Calvez & J. Perrin *Eglise et société économique* (Paris 1959); R. Coste *Morale internationale* (Paris-Tournai 1964); R. Bosc *La société internationale et l'Eglise* (Paris 1968).

3. P. Haubtmann 'La communauté humaine' in *Vatican II, l'Eglise dans le monde de ce temps* vol II *Commentaires* (Paris 1967) p. 275.

4. See P. Antoine 'Les droits de l'homme ont-ils changé de sens?' and J.-Y. Calvez 'Nouveauté des droits de l'homme dans "Pacem in terris"' in *Revue de l'Action Populaire* No. 174 (January 1964) pp. 3-18, 40-56. See pp. 50-56 for the parallels between the Universal Declaration of 1948 and *Pacem in terris.*

5. Cf. Y. Congar 'Le role de l'Eglise dans le monde de ce temps' in *Vatican II, L'Eglise dans le monde de ce temps* vol. II pp. 305 ff.

6. Quoted by R. Coste *op. cit.* p. 231.

7. P. Haubtmann *op. cit.* pp. 256-260.

8. See *Document de travail* of the commission *Justitia et Pax.*

9. See the dossier gathered together in *Pro Mundi Vita* (Bulletin No. 71 March-April 1978).

10. P. Valadier 'La reference à l'ecriture en morale politique' in *Ecriture et pratique chrétienne* (Coll. Lectio divina 96) (Paris 1978) p. 183. See also the current debates provoked by President Carter's policies.

11. Mgr. Casaroli 'Le Saint-siège entre les tensions et la détente' in *Documentation catholique* (16th April 1978) col. 380.

12. B. Dupuy 'La force et la fragilité' in *Istina* (1978) No. 2-3, 119. The same number reproduces the contribution made by Mgr. Silvestrini at the Belgrade Conference.

Leopold J. Niilus

Efforts for Human Rights of The World Council of Churches and of S.O.D.E.P.A.X.

THE WORLD Council of Churches (W.C.C.) as an institution cannot be properly defined as a 'Church's Central Administration'. In accordance with its Constitution, the W.C.C. is a *fellowship of churches*. The W.C.C. constituency has an essential bearing on its human rights' efforts. A world fellowship of nearly 300 churches, Protestant, Anglican Orthodox, in over 90 countries—North, South, East and West—enables it to bring together persons from different tradition and differing political, economic and cultural situations. Yet all united in Christ and thus, through their common allegiance and mutual trust able to share openly their agreements and disagreements, and so by genuine dialogue learn from one another.

Among the W.C.C. *functions and purposes*, stated in its constitution, clearly also relevant for human rights concerns, we note the call 'to facilitate the common concern of the churches in the service of human need, the breaking down of barriers between people, and the promotion of one human family in justice and peace'. The W.C.C. has the authority to 'offer counsel and provide opportunity for united action in matters of common interest', but it 'shall not legislate for the churches; nor shall it act for them . . .'.

1. LOCAL/UNIVERSAL

The W.C.C. human rights' efforts therefore need to be seen in the light of a dialectical relationship between two poles: the local/congregational and the universal/ecumenical.

In an ecumenical fellowship it is basically the member churches, where they live and witness, who are expected and called to take matters in their hands, establish their own policies, also in regard to the implementation and protection of human rights. The universal itself needs the local. 'One of the ways of creating greater awareness and understanding of the world situation is through awareness and understanding of one's own national situation, and of its relations to the situations of other nations in an interdependent world.'[1]

At the same time, in a fellowship of *churches*, the universal dimension must be kept constantly present. And especially so where human rights are concerned. 'The emphasis of the Gospel is on the value of all human beings in the sight of God, on the atoning and redeeming work of Christ that has given to humanity true dignity, on love for one's neighbour as the practical expression of an active faith in Christ. We are members one of another, and when one suffers all are hurt.'[1] 'Our chief task is to work for the realization of (human rights) *where we are*, but when there are those elsewhere who are powerless to cry out, we are called to be the voice of the voiceless and the advocates of the oppressed.'[2]

In this whole context the practical point of view of efficiency is relevant as well. The W.C.C. Central Committee in Addis Ababa, 1971,[3] indicated as one of the man emphases for W.C.C's human rights efforts the need to 'relate standards of human rights to the cultural, socio-economic and political settings of different parts of the world . . . emphasis being laid on finding more effective means of international co-operation for the implementation of human rights'. Implementation of human rights within those different settings clearly tells us that in the last analysis effective action by the churches depends upon the response of local congregations.

We also need to avoid the trap of earlier misconceptions of 'missionary activity', which was based on a mentality of donor and receiver. 'We' went 'overseas' to do things 'for them'. Some of that attitude still lingers on *vis-à-vis* certain human rights' conceptions in the industrially developed West: 'We', who have no real human rights' problems to face and enjoy all the freedom to 'dissent', need to straighten out human rights 'for them', 'overseas' or 'out there'. Legitimate concepts of *ecumenical solidarity* and *mutual enabling* are of a different kind. Lest we are led to fragmentation and narrow vision, the local and concrete must be brought together, broadened and challenged against a world perspective. Need will also arise 'to be the voice of the voiceless and the advocates of the oppressed'. But here great care must be taken not to act unwisely out of self-righteousness or even arrogance.

2. INTERRELATEDNESS

In our present world human rights' violations increasingly reflect alarming trends of *globality* and *interrelatedness*. If ever there was a time when most human rights' violations occurred in one part of the world only (and this very assumption is in itself a most dubious one), then this certainly is no longer the case. In regard to the *interrelatedness* of human rights, it is twofold. The St Pölten Consultation earlier referred to, underlined that all human rights, be they social, economic, religious or political are intertwined and interrelated and need to be taken as a whole. But the interrelatedness of all human rights was seen not only in terms of categories and substance but also geographically. In today's world some of the interlinkages are so dangerous that they could be deemed to be qualitatively new. Peace researchers have expressed the strongest concern about the following interrelated spheres: (*a*) the accelerated arms' race; (*b*) the widening disparity between rich and poor in the global society; (*c*) the growing wave of oppression, authoritarian rule and contempt for human rights in a majority of world nations. These three circles converge and reinforce each other. Armaments and militarism obstruct development; denial of human rights truncates development and serves to feed and sustain militarism. All three meet in breeding violence and represent an acute threat to humanity and peace.

Another most alarming aspect besides the globality of human rights' violations is the fact that these violations tend to become increasing *standardised*. The highest 'visibility' of this phenomenon is found in the field of torture. In our generation the imhumanity of torture is becoming a more widespread and atrocious reality than at any other time in history. Equally alarming is the frightening existence of an international commerce in torture techniques and equipment and the overt or covert development in the scientific community of even more sophisticated techniques of physical and psychological torture.[4]

In working for human rights we are often tempted to deal with symptoms rather than root causes. While we must work for the abolition of specific denials of human rights, much more awareness is needed in regard to situations which generate human rights' violations and their growing evil interrelatedness. Any glib assumption about 'evil out there' and safe havens 'at home' is today dangerously misleading. Trends towards suppression of differing opinions and erosion of civil liberties is growingly evident, if less openly brutal, in industrialised nations as well. Violation of civil liberties in the name of 'national security' by means of infiltration into peace and human rights' organisations by intelligence agencies, the use of electronic surveillance in private homes and headquarters of political and social organisations, and the maintenance of computerised government files on the total life patterns of individuals, indicate the degree to which human rights and political freedom are being sacrificed everywhere.[5]

Today's globality and interrelatedness of human rights confronts us with a *methodological challenge* as well. The very concept of 'human rights' in its present use has ceased to be basically a 'scientific subject' because it is increasingly becoming too vague and all inclusive. Yet because of this very fact the real strength of the term lies today in its moral force. The quest for human rights has become essentially a call for *a new type of international morality*. In this regard one specific W.C.C. main programme emphasis should be noticed here, namely the search for a 'Just, Participatory and Sustainable Society (J.P.S.S.)'. All these insights and thrusts should be seen as background for W.C.C's institutional efforts and *modus operandi* in the field of human rights.[6]

3. INSTITUTIONAL EFFORTS

Symptons and root causes: A concerted effort to perceive human rights in terms of processes seeking ways and means to counteract and overcome situations which maintain and generate human rights' violations has manifold implications. It has become increasingly important to operate on long range pedagogical lines: to uncover, create awareness, learn from one another, create effectiveness. As there is a constant danger of falling into the trap of simple activism the emphasis needs to be put on the interrelatedness of the various rights, the work for the elimination of root causes, and to plan actions which are appropriate to the situations addressed. Churches should guard against a simplistic, activist approach which divorces action from reflection.

A growing programmatic involvement of the churches in the field of human rights has also caused that many of the W.C.C. programme sub-units have highlighted human rights aspects of their ongoing work or taken them up as a part of their programme focus. Current W.C.C. programme activities, besides the central programme thrusts on human rights by the Commission of the Churches on International Affairs (C.C.I.A.), can be grouped under the following categories:[7]

Support of churches, groups and networks engaged concretely: Primarily involved here are the Commission on Inter-Church Aid, Refugee and World Service (C.I.C.A.R.W.S.) area desks, Urban and Industrial Mission (U.I.M.) in the Commission on World Mission and Evangelism (C.W.M.E.), the Human Rights Resource Office for Latin America (H.R.R.O.L.A.), the regional task forces, the Migrations Desk, the Programme to Combat Racism (P.C.R.), the Commission on the Churches' Participation in Development (C.C.P.D.) and C.C.I.A. Most often these tasks involve co-ordination with regional ecumenical bodies concerned.

Mobilisation of the Churches' resources to combat violations of human rights in various parts of the world: C.I.C.A.R.W.S., P.C.R. and the W.C.C. Unit II H.R.R.O.L.A. are deeply involved in mobilising both financial, personnel and solidarity resources for that continent. The Refugee Service of C.I.C.A.R.W.S. brings resources of the churches to bear on the protection of growing numbers of refugees in the world. C.C.I.A. mobilises non-financial resources.

Serving as a communications centre and information-gathering and disseminating body: Frequently the W.C.C. is a privileged recipient of rapid information about specific violations of human rights involving individuals and groups, and of more analytical studies of situations in which human rights are violated. The various sub-units and staff regional task forces have established networks in the churches to which this information is transmitted, along with requests for specific supportive actions.

Awareness building and education on human rights: The Christian Medical Commission (C.M.C.), in the field of human rights and health-care; the sub-unit on Women, in relation to women's programme in the churches and the special plight of women in repressive situations; C.W.M.E., in relationship to the mission and witness of the church; C.C.P.D., in terms, particularly, of economic and social justice; P.C.R., in the field of racial justice; H.R.R.O.L.A. in relation to violations of human rights in Latin America; C.C.I.A. in connection with the international aspects of national or regional human rights problems.

S.O.D.E.P.A.X.: Through S.O.D.E.P.A.X., the joint W.C.C./Roman Catholic Committee on Society, Development and Peace, the W.C.C. and the Roman Catholic Church work together on questions of justice and peace. As the W.C.C. 1977 report on human rights indicated, especially in the field of awareness-building and education on human rights S.O.D.E.P.A.X. is engaged here in relation to its programme 'Towards a New Society', and in this and other above mentioned areas, served as a direct link to the Pontifical Commission Justice and Peace of the Roman Catholic Church. Appeals in human rights' matters are forwarded to the W.C.C. and the Holy See for appropriate action, since S.O.D.E.P.A.X. is not empowered to act directly in such cases. It acts as a channel of liaison between the C.C.I.A. of the W.C.C. and the Pontifical Commission Justice and Peace of the Holy See, in order to promote exchange of information on human rights situations and sharing of viewpoints on the role of the churches in protecting human rights. S.O.D.E.P.A.X. has attempted to initiate an ecumenical dialogue on the theological basis of human rights at its Colloquium on Recent Developments in the Social Thinking of the Churches, held at Rocca di Papa, Italy, in July 1977, and in subsequent liaison efforts, together with C.C.I.A., aimed at protecting a multilateral study project on this question among the W.C.C. and several of the largest world confessional families.

Notes

1. *Human Rights and Christian Responsibility* Report of the Consultation, St Pölten, Austria, October 1974 (C.C.I.A./W.C.C., Geneva).
2. W.C.C. Fifth Assembly, (Nairobi, Kenya 1975), *Structures of Injustice and Struggles for Liberation* (W.C.C., Geneva).
3. W.C.C. Central Committee, (Addis Ababa, 1971), *Report and Recommendations on Human Rights* (W.C.C., Geneva).
4. W.C.C. Central Committee, (Geneva, 1977), *Statement on Torture* (C.C.I.A./W.C.C., Geneva).
5. *Report of the Consultation on Militarism,* Glion, Switzerland, November, 1977, and *Report of the Conference on Disarmament*, Glion, Switzerland, April, 1978 (C.C.I.A./W.C.C., Geneva).
6. See above, as well as W.C.C. Central Committee, (Geneva, 1976), *Recommendations on Human Rights*, and W.C.C. Central Committee, (Geneva, 1977), *Report on Human Rights* (C.C.I.A./W.C.C., Geneva).
7. For overall historical reference, see *Religious Freedom: Main Statements by the World Council of Churches 1948-1975* (C.C.I.A./W.C.C., Geneva).

Maria Goretti and Domingo Sale

The Church and the Human Rights Struggle in the Philippines

THOUGH the Catholic Church claims the allegiance of 85 per cent of the people in the Philippines, one cannot say it is united in its stand on human rights. In a statement issued on 4th November 1976, seventeen bishops addressed themselves to the main source of this division, 'the martial law government for which basic human rights are of secondary importance'.[1] In this brief article, we shall try to sketch a history of the Church and the human rights struggle in the Philippines over the past six years.

1. POLITICAL DETAINEES

In February 1977, the Secretary of National Defense admitted that some 60,000 persons had been arrested since the beginning of martial law.[2] Few of these have ever been charged and with the exception of Senator Benigno Aquino, Victor Corpuz and Bernabe Buscayno, none has ever been sentenced. Two reports of the Major Superiors of Religious Men and Women of the Philippines as well as the Report of the Amnesty International Mission to the Philippines in November and a more recent report of the International Commission of Jurists document extensive use of torture on political detainees as well as a good number of deaths due to torture.[3] In recent months outside pressure on the Marcos government to respect human rights has simply led to the disappearance of those apprehended immediately after their arrest. The recent discovery of a mass grave in Mauban, Quezon, in which the bodies of a number of people known to have been apprehended in Manila were found is evidence enough of what is happening in such disappearances.[4]

Though the seventeen bishops mentioned above and the Task Force of the Major Superiors on Political detainees have continued to document and speak out strongly against arbitrary arrests,[5] detention and torture of political detainees, the Catholic Bishops' Conference has failed to do so, despite a number of requests to issue a statement on political detainees and their treatment.

2. LABOUR

In November 1975, the first successful strike under martial law was held in the La Tondeña distillery in Manila. This was met by Presidential Decree 823 which banned all strikes and prohibited any support of any kind to workers in their organisation and action for justice.[6] This prohibition was clearly aimed at religious and priests who were active in the cause of labour. Cardinal Sin, Archbishop of Manila, along with 2,000 bishops, priests and religious sent a letter to the President 'vigorously protesting' the decree. To silence the protest, a few changes were made in the wording of the decree but the substance remains unchanged and the decree remains in effect.[7]

3. AGRICULTURAL TENANTS AND LABOURERS

Perhaps even worse off than the urban industrial workers at present are the agricultural tenants and labourers. At the beginning of martial law, President Marcos issued a Land Reform Decree to cover tenants on all rice and corn lands of 7 hectares and above. He claimed at the time the success or failure of his administration would be judged by the implementation of land reform. Shortly after the decree was issued many land owners converted their rice and corn lands to other crops, others merely moved tenants off the land and employed them as agricultural labourers, still others converted their lands into housing subdivisions. Soon after the law was passed but without changing the law itself, the President set the retention limit at 24 hectares rather than 7 thus excluding from Land Reform over 60 per cent of all tenants.[8]

4. CULTURAL MINORITIES

While Land Reform was being proclaimed by the government, ancestral lands of the cultural minorities were being fraudulently expropriated for the multinational fruit companies such as Del Monte and Dole. In other cases lands were taken over by the government for hydro-electric dam sites to benefit large export oriented land holders.[9] In many areas of Mindanao, small landowners were also forced to lease their lands to the big fruit companies through fraud and deception or intimidation by the military.[10]

While some priests and sisters and the seventeen bishops mentioned earlier have been closely identified with the cause of urban and agricultural workers and tenants and with the cultural minorities, the Catholic Bishops' Conference has to date issued only one statement on the plight of the cultural minorities. But beyond the statement little has happened by way of active support either for the people themselves or for these priests and religious working with them.

5. GOVERNMENT ATTACKS

In September 1976, a series of articles appeared in the local press, attacking priests and religious working with the poor. The effort was to discredit them by linking them to the Communist Party.[11] The campaign was shrewdly managed. While the campaign was being waged in the Press, bishops sympathetic to the government were shown films, fabricated by the Government Information Office and given briefings aimed at creating the impression of an imminent threat to the government and the Church. Again, the seventeen bishops wrote a strong letter to the editors of the local press to protest the attempt to caricature those working with the poor as 'Communist'. Though the campaign abated somewhat, it still continues in more subtle ways.

6. REFERENDUM

On 11th December 1974 President Marcos announced the third referendum under martial law. Six weeks before the referendum scheduled for 27th February 1975 the Mindanao-Sulu Secretariat for Social Action issued a Manifesto on boycotting the referendum stating that unless Martial Law is lifted, and free discussion is permitted, 'we cannot allow ourselves to participate in another mockery of Democracy'. Recognising that Martial Law would not be lifted and hence that free discussion could not take place the Manifesto concluded: 'Our consciences compel us to boycott the forthcoming referendum.' A few days later this Manifesto was endorsed by the Major Superiors of Religious.[13]

At their annual meeting in late January 1975, the Catholic Bishops' Conference of the Philippines issued a statement on the referendum. While not endorsing a boycott, the bishops asked for 'free public discussion of the issues, freedom of speech, of peaceful assembly and of all media' so that 'every citizen has the opportunity to freely express his views'. They did not, however, request the lifting of Martial Law. Finally, they 'suggested' to the President that for this referendum he suspend the penalties against those who fail to vote, or abstain from voting, and openly express their stand.[14] The C.B.C.P. seemed to recognise a boycott as a moral option and so the letter was interpreted. However, as referendum day approached, many of the bishops went on record as opposing a boycott, one even went to the extent of threatening a group of sisters with excommunication unless they voted. The seventeen bishops did point out to their people in sermons and through letters that a boycott in the present situation was a moral option. Though the Press kept minimising the boycott threat and predicting no more than 2 per cent of the voters would boycott, the actual number boycotting was closer to 25 per cent.[15]

The issue of the boycott highlighted the division in the Church and prepared the stage for Rome to intervene.

7. ROME INTERVENES

On 17th April 1975 the Chairman of Associations of Religious Men and Women each received a letter from the late Cardinal Tabera, Prefect of the Sacred Congregation of Religious.[16] This letter was coursed through the Nunciature. The Cardinal expressed worry over the 'unfortunate turn of events of the past several months in connection with the Association of Major Religious Superiors'.[17] The letter went on to criticise 'the almost exclusively socio-political emphasis of the association which obscures the spiritual idea of Apostolic, religious life'.[18] At the request of the Superiors, a meeting was held with the Apostolic Nuncio on 10th May 1975 to discuss the letters of Cardinal Tabera. At this meeting, it was clear to the Superiors that 'the rather unfortunate turn of events' and 'almost exclusively socio-political emphasis' referred to was the referendum. The Nuncio considered the referendum 'per se', a *purely* political issue.[19] On another occasion, the Nuncio stated the letters were sent in an effort to preserve the unity that should exist among bishops and between bishops and religious.[20] This unity was made to appear as an absolute to be preserved at all costs even the cost of ignoring clear violations of human rights. Within a year, the Chairman of the Association of Religious Women was declared inelligible for re-election as Provincial of her Congregation and the Chairman of the Association of Religious Men was ordered by Rome to leave the country for one year.

8. C.B.C.P. EFFORTS TO APPEASE GOVERNMENT

At the meeting of the Catholic Bishops' Conference held in July 1975, with one exception, a pro-government Board was elected to head the Bishops' Conference for the next two years. Immediately after their election, though not scheduled to take office till January 1976, the new Board met with President Marcos. This meeting caused considerable embarrassment in Church circles when the day after the meeting, the

Press carried the headline, 'Catholic Church, traditional foe of birth control, restated its agreement yesterday with President Marcos' basic policy that government would support all family planning methods'.[21] When, on the following day Cardinal Rosales, the new President of the Conference, issued a clarification, it was carried in an obscure section of the Press. The Cardinal's statement merely added to the confusion by giving the impression that the Church had substantially changed her stand on *Humanae Vitae*.[22]

After the summary deportation of four priests in late 1975 and early 1976, the Board of the C.B.C.P. tried to block discussion of this matter at the January 1976 meeting of the Conference. Eventually they agreed to investigate the deportation. Rather than investigate, however, they settled for the word of the President that justice was done. This led some of the seventeen bishops to charge the board with having made a deal with the President. The evidence seems to support this charge.[23]

In January 1977 after the military had closed down two Church radio stations and three publications, the Bishops' Conference issued a rather surprising pastoral letter in which they spoke diplomatically but with a certain firmness on the basic rights of families, tribal minorities, workers for evangelisation and the right of due process.[24] The more progressive bishops encouraged by this statement felt that the new Board to be elected at the July 1977 meeting, would be much more representative of the entire Conference. That was not to be. In July, the pro-government group within the Conference came with a prepared slate of candidates which they succeeded in having elected. At this meeting too, the Bishops' Conference refused to face the issue of widespread abuses of human rights in the government's Family Planning Programme.

9. RECENT ELECTIONS

In April 1978, the country held its first election under Martial Law. The results when announced were a complete victory for all government candidates. However, the massive and well documented cases of fraud, especially in the Greater Manila area, cast serious doubts on the proclaimed victory of the government candidates.[25] Two days after the elction in a peaceful march to protest the conduct of the election, over 500 people were arrested including four opposition candidates, two former Senators, one priest and six sisters. Two days after the march, the military visited four religious houses, one of them was raided. A young man arrested in this raid was dead four days later as the result of torture.[26] The Major Religious Superiors called for a day of prayer and fasting at the Manila Cathedral to protest at all these events. But the Bishops as a body have up to now been silent.

10. CONCLUSION

There is little indication at present that the Bishops' Conference will take a more forceful stand on human rights. They fear the consequences of not going along with the government, taxation of Church property, control of Catholic schools and other forms of harassment. These threats are real. They have been made from time to time. The sad fact is they have silenced the voice of the Bishops' Conference on issues of human rights. Recently, when about to leave for Rome, Cardinal Sin was delayed by the military at the airport in an attempt to prevent him from leaving the country.[27] The Nuncio raised the matter with the President. An apology was issued.[28] Yet the Nuncio's voice along with that of the Bishops' Conference has been mute in the face of arbitrary arrests and detention, the torture and killings of political detainees, the inhuman uprooting of poor squatters, land-grabbing, rampant disregard of the rights of cultural minorities and the continued repression and harrassment of industrial workers in their attempts to express legitimate grievances. The Conference has failed to speak either on gross disregard of the freedoms of speech and peaceful assembly and on the right of access to information. It would seem that for the Nuncio and the majority of bishops, the overriding consideration is preserving the privileges of the institutional Church.

On the other hand the seventeen bishops along with a good number of priests and religious will continue to speak out in defence of human rights. For them the Church's concern for justice cannot remain remote from the daily experiences of people. The situation in the dioceses of these bishops reflects their concern. Their people are active in the life of the Church. They are overcoming their fears and speaking out on, as well as organising themselves to confront, issues of justice and human rights.

In a sense, there are two Churches in the Philippines at present, the old institution-based, establishment-oriented Church seeking to preserve *what is*, and the new, dynamic people-oriented Church which is reaching out to the 80 per cent of the people who are poor and oppressed and who have, up to now, been largely neglected by the institutional Church. The dynamism of this new Church is responding to the simple but deep faith of the poor and in the process releasing hitherto untapped resources. More and more the little people are reading the signs of the times in their own lives and in the world around them in the light of faith. Their simple reflections are deep and moving. They are articulating in their own way a truly, indigenuous theology and finding their own identity as an authentically local Church. The simplicity, honesty and directness of their approach is perhaps the greatest threat to the old establishment based Church and to the martial law regime.

At this point the Church is split on the issue of human rights. One view sees this as a bad thing. Another view recognising God's providence in human affairs and realising that the Paschal Mystery is part of every human endeavour sees it as challenge to growth. At present this new Church is small. It is a suffering Church but it is growing strong and fearless. Traditionally, it has been said the blood of the martyrs is the seed of the Church. Today, the poor, suffering and, in many cases, dying in defence of their dignity and the dignity of their fellow men, are bearing witness to their faith in the living God, active in history and in His son, Jesus Christ, who died that all men might live. They are as much martyrs as the martyrs of old for through their blood, they are seeding this new, dynamic, vital Church of the poor.

Notes

1. *Ut Omnes Unum Sint.* Statement of seventeen bishops, 4th November 1977.

2. Statement made by the Secretary of National Defense Juan Ponce Enrile on B.B.C. Documentary *Collision Course*. Shown on B.B.C., (9th May 1977).

3. *Political Detainees in the Philippines* (A.M.R.S.P., Manila: 31st March 1976 and 1977); *Report of an Amnesty International Mission to the Republic of the Philippines,* 22nd November-5th December 1975 (London: A.I., 1976, 2nd edition, 1977); *The Decline of Democracy in the Philippines* (Geneva: International Commission of Jurists, 1977).

4. *Political Detainees Update*, (30th September 1977).

5. The Task Force of the Major Superiors issues periodic reports on detainees. These reports contain data on recent arrests, cases of torture and death, and updates on the number of detainees.

6. *Justice for the Filipino Worker* (Manila: A.M.R.S.P., 1976). The letter of Cardinal Sin on P.D. 823, the decree itself and other data are found in this pamphlet.

7. *Ibid.*

8. *Signs of the Times*, passim. The publication of the A.M.R.S.P. was raided and closed by the military on 5th December 1976.

9. *Ibid.* passim.

10. *Ibid.* passim.

11. *Times Journal*, 1st September 1976; *Bulletin Today*, 1st September 1976; *Philippines Daily Express*, 9th September 1976, 16th September 1976 among others.

12. 'Letter to Editor, Times Journal, Bulletin Today, Philippine Daily Express.' The letter was undated. This letter was never published in the Press.

13. Manifesto of the Mindanao-Sulu Secretariat for Social Action (M.I.S.S.A.), 9th January 1975. The endorsement of the Major Superiors is appended to the Manifesto.

14. Statement of the Catholic Bishops' Conference on the Referendum signed for the C.B.C.P. by Julio Cardinal Rosales, President, and dated 3rd January 1976.

15. *Signs of the Times*, March 1976 presents an analysis of the voting results. The government itself claimed there were 24 million registered voters. Later it said about 18 million voted in the referendum.

16. Letters addressed to Sister Christine Tan, R.G.S., and the Rev. Beningo A. Mayo, S.J., signed by Cardinal Tabera and dated 17th April 1976. The letters were identical.

17. *Ibid.*

18. *Ibid.*

19. The Superiors issued a summary report of this meeting dated 24th June 1975.

20. Interview given by Mgr. Torpigliani, the Apostolic Nuncio, on 25th May 1977 in Malaybalay, Bukidnon.

21. *Bulletin Today*, July 1975.

22. *Ibid.*

23. Letter of Bishop Jesus Varela to Cardinal Rosales dated 2nd April 1976 and the reply of Cardinal Rosales to Bishop Varela, *Signs of the Times,* 1st May 1976.

24. Pastoral letter of Catholic Bishops' Conference to the People of God, dated 29th January 1977.

25. *Ichthys* 28th April 1978.

26. *Ichthys* 12th May 1978 and 9th June 1978.

27. *Bulletin Today* 21st May to 28th May 1978.

28. *Ibid.*

Segundo Galilea

The Church in Latin America and the Struggle for Human Rights

1. A FACT OF EVERYDAY PASTORAL CONCERN

THE FIGHT for human rights in Latin America has in recent years become such an everyday aspect of the Church's pastoral activity on the sub-continent that it has come to be identified with her understanding of her mission to mankind. This fight goes on in every country; either at the level of local Christian communities or at a level which has achieved greater popular acclaim, viz. that of the national hierarchies—apart from four or five exceptions.

This 'pastoral action for human rights' is not limited to statements and condemnations, it also takes the form of specific commitments, organised activities and in several countries has been established on a permanent basis. One of the best known examples of this is the *Vicaria de la Solidaridad* (Vicariate for Common Action) in Chile, which assumed responsibility for the human and legal requirements of the dispossessed, political prisoners, people who had been sacked or were unemployed and vast numbers of the extremely poor. A similar organisation in Bolivia is the *Asamblea de los Derechos Humanos* (Congress for Human Rights) and in Brazil several organisations committed to the principle of non-violence have come into being, perhaps the best known of which is the *Campaña de la Fraternidad* (Campaign for Brotherhood). All of these organisations depend on the support of the hierarchy. Others which ought to be added to this list include organisations like *Iglesia Solidaria* (Church of Solidarity) in Peru and Mexico which unite groups of priests, religious and laity in common action with the hierarchy. Furthermore, ordinary people have bonded together into ecclesial communities which have become forums for liberty and the defence of justice in areas where every other form of organisation at this level is restricted.

A measure of the significance of the Church's activity on behalf of human rights is that it has created one of the outstanding aspects of Latin American Christianity in this decade: persecution. It is practised openly or in secret, it can be physical or psychological and is the tool of governments and the traditionally privileged classes. Persecution is never 'official' in countries which have a Catholic tradition. It is carried out with skill and discretion, above all against the most vulnerable sections of society and often by those most committed to the cause of the liberation of the oppressed.

Persecution creates martyrs; not necessarily in the canonical sense but in a wider and equally authentic sense—Christians who, motivated by their faith, have given their lives in the cause of justice.[1] Although the Churches in Latin America have suffered sporadic persecutions since the independence of their respective countries, persecution takes a different form nowadays because it originates from the Church's active support of human rights, and not from her defence of her own rights as happened in the nineteenth century. Accordingly, the bishops and Christian communities involved in the contemporary struggle for human rights are following the traditions of the sixteenth century when many missionaries fought for the rights of the natives throughout the whole of America.

Several social and ecclesial factors combine to make the present struggle a 'sign of the times'.

1. Over the past twenty years or so the Latin American people have become increasingly aware of the oppression imposed on the majority of the population. Their liberation is a human right which cannot be ignored and the Church, basing herself on the Gospels and her missionary responsibilities, obviously shares this view.

2. The Second Vatican Council stressed the Church's function of servant of mankind. This change of ecclesiological emphasis was made relevant to Latin America at the Episcopal Conference of Medellín (1968) which declared the Church's commitment to fight for the rights and liberation of the poorest and most deprived of her children.

3. This new awareness on the part of the Church posed a threat to the 'established order'. And one result of this latent conflict was the proliferation of oppressive regimes in South America, which, by their very nature, have aggravated the human rights' problem and highlighted the fact that it is such a fundamental issue. Furthermore, in every Latin American country today, the extent to which the people can exercise their rights is systematically controlled in one way or another. With varying degrees of emphasis, the defence of National Security is the prevailing concern of every government, even in Cuba, although reasons and

methods vary there from the rest of Latin America. The social and moral burden which the Church in South America has to bear leaves her little choice between God and Caesar, Moses and Pharaoh.

4. This hardening of political attitudes brought about the eventual downfall of the popular and political elite along with the leaders of the worker and peasant organisations. In these circumstances, the Church—but especially the hierarchy—has become the only line of defence of the rights of the oppressed. The Church is now the 'voice of those who have no voice', and consequently very many bishops are involved in this campaign.

2. BETWEEN GOD AND CAESAR

One major factor in the Latin American Church's fight for human rights is the increasing volume in most countries of episcopal statements on this issue. Virtually every time the bishops speak on temporal matters, they refer to the human rights' problem. Perhaps the only other similar case is that of the Church in South Africa which has to confront the racialist problems of that country.

There is no regular pattern to the scope and strength of the attitudes adopted in these circumstances because the extent to which human rights are repressed varies so much according to time and place. The response of some hierarchies to the problem is just as varied—there are even those who believe that Christians who fight for human rights are simply playing into the hands of the communists!

I shall look briefly at the statements and activities of Episcopal Conferences over the past two years[2] with particular reference to what is most relevant while not forgetting that individual bishops, priests, religious and lay people have been equally active. The whole world knows the attitudes adopted by Dom Helder, Dom Proaño and the Cardinals of Sâo Paolo, Lima, Santiago and La Paz in defending the oppressed in specific instances.

On June 12th 1976 the bishops of Paraguay stood up to the government and condemned its systematic repression not just of public and political freedom but also of peasant organisations, many of which are encouraged by priests. The elimination of the leaders of the people forces priests to help in guiding the peasant and worker organisations in many parts of the sub-continent; and this is only one area of conflict in the Church's struggle for the rights of the poor.

In June 1976 the hierarchy of Bolivia openly supported a strike by impoverished tin-miners. This was not the first occasion, as the Church in Bolivia has a long tradition of fighting for miners' rights. In December of the same year the bishops condemned the living standards and lack of liberty of the Bolivian people.

In Guatemala the problems of human rights and justice came to a head in the wake of an earthquake which struck the country. In August 1976 the bishops published a letter, *Unidos en la Esperanza* (United in Hope), which proved profoundly prophetic.

On October 4th 1976 the bishops of Peru stated in their letter *Justicia en el mundo* (Justice in the World) that human rights are more important than the re-organisation of the economy, no matter the cost. In fact, the problem of development programmes which sacrifice the rights of the weak has been a constant theme in statements by hierarchies and other organisations within the Church in Latin America.

It is probably in Brazil that the Church has had the longest and most conflict-ridden struggle for the rights of the weak. It has been an uneven struggle because the hierarchy which is numerous represents a broad spectrum of opinion. Just as in Chile and Uruguay, the Brazilian bishops have had to confront a strong government committed to maintaining National Security. Despite the granting of relative freedom in this country the bishops recently had to intervene twice in the same six months. In 'A Pastoral Letter to the People of God' (November 1976) the hierarchy point out the ideological roots of the arbitrary decisions made by those in power and the oppression they impose. Four months later they spoke out in defence of personal, public and economic liberty in *Lineamentos para un orden político* (Guidelines for Political Order).

In Nicaragua where violation of human rights reached tyrannical proportions the bishops, who wavered for decades, finally broke with Somoza, condemning the lack of liberty and the minimal rights of the population. This happened in January 1977 and was an important stage in the regime's decline, although the government initially censured the bishop's action.

El Salvador is a small country controlled by a coterie of land-owners who work hand in glove with the government. Here, as in other places, the rights of man are the rights of the peasants. For some time now official pastoral policy—especailly that of the Jesuits—has supported agrarian reform and peasant organisation. This policy unleashed one of the fiercest persecutions in recent years in Latin America. On March 5th 1977 the bishops stood up in defence of the peasant organisations, the militants and the priests who were being persecuted, and condemned the repressive and unjust state of affairs.

In Chile the problem of human rights has turned relations between Church and state at all levels into a series of conflicts. The bishops took up the cause of dispossessed peasants (July 11th 1977) and oppressed workers (May 1st 1978). On March 23rd 1977 they challenged the government to lay down a basic standard of life for the whole nation.

Finally, in November 1977 the bishops who served on the Latin

American Commission for Non-violent Action published the most decisive and coherent document on the rights of the poor since the Conference of Medellín, which provides Christian guide-lines for non-violent action.

A great deal more could be said. As I have already indicated, persecution and martyrdom have often been the price paid for this kind of attitude, more so at the bottom than at the top of society. Enough has already occurred to change the secular relationship between the powers that be and the Catholic Church.

The most outstanding incident happened in August 1977 when seventeen Latin American bishops were arrested and virtually expelled from Ecuador; their crime was collective criticism in the face of the peasant situation. In El Salvador catechists and religious have been assassinated; the same happened in Honduras where the massacre of Olancho (June 25th 1975) stirred the conscience of the whole Church in South America. In all of these cases the rights of the peasants who were being exploited was the point at issue. It is well known that priests and vicars episcopal have been imprisoned and put to death in the Argentine, Uruguay and Brazil. Missionaries have been expelled *en masse* from Central America, Chile, Brazil, Bolivia, Paraguay, the Argentine, Cuba and more sporadically from other countries in the sub-continent. It goes without saying that this has not always been on account of Christ, his Church and the poor. The pastoral mission of some persecuted churchmen has sometimes been ambiguous, misdirected, lacking coherence and in many cases coloured by political bias. Not all 'prophets' are genuine. What is important is the over-all reality; as for the rest, ambiguity has always been an aspect of religious persecution.

3. HUMAN RIGHTS, THE RIGHTS OF THE POOR

At least in regard to Latin America, one can point out some of the pastoral and ecclesial significance of all these facts.

1. Here, as in the rest of the Third World, the question of human rights has reached such proportions that for the majority it has become the basic problem of 'being human', and an institutionalised social sin for the attention of the Church. Progress and liberation in Latin America are both ethical and pastoral problems.

2. The Church's struggle for human rights is not primarily concerned with public, political and intellectual liberty but with the basic rights of workers, peasants and natives. In contrast to these basically 'human' rights, the right to dissent and the right to a free Press are luxuries. In

Latin America we are dealing with the right to work, to earn a minimum wage, to be fed, to acquire a basic education, not to live in permanent insecurity, not to be systematically deprived and discriminated against and to have workers' organisations. In Latin America, the rights of man are the rights of the poor.

3. In general terms, as the Church has fulfilled this particular mission she has deepened her roots amongst the people and is gradually taking on the appearance of a Church of the poor. This, however, is not the case over-all, although it is becoming such in many parts of the sub-continent. It is above all a challenge to effectively realise the conciliar ideal of 'the Church of the poor' and as such Latin America offers a privileged opportunity; it is a continent of poor people where the Church is still relevant.

4. The struggle for the rights of the poor, without discrimination, creates a missionary perspective for the Church's pastoral activity, and offers the possibility of concerted action with individuals, groups and ideologies traditionally hostile to the Church. In this regard what has happened in Chile is very significant: the fact that the Church supported Marxists who were persecuted and deprived, with all the consequences that this implied, showed those groups the non-sectarianism and freely-given service of a Church which they did not know. In Chile and in other countries, non-believers now accept that the Church is no longer an institution behind which Capitalism can hide, and that it is not 'the opium of the people'.

5. The struggle for the rights of the poor is improving relations between the Church and society in Latin America. The historico-traditional relations of the Catholic Church and society could be defined by the equation Church-State where the predominant preoccupation of the clergy was always relations with the government. Until relatively recently, the eventual conflicts were generated by politico-ecclesiastical problems. Nowadays, no one believes that the Church's main interest should be her relationship with governments but rather her relationship with the people, and on this account the Church finds herself in opposition to the State. In those areas where relations between government and people have seriously deteriorated because of human rights, a Church at the service of her people has to be free and assume a prophetic role of opposition to the state, if she does not wish to run the risk of losing all relevance amongst the people. The Church's struggle for human rights—for the rights of the poor—is a door to liberty and a means of fulfilling her prophetic mission.

6. This situation still contains serious difficulties. For example, the hopes of the poor can be frustrated and this is to the detriment of the spread of the Gospel. This is already happening where official groups

within the Church have not adopted a clearly defined stance or where real or apparent progress has not been made, because evangelisation in Latin America depends more on solving the problems of justice rather than the problems created by secularisation.

In a situation in which the hierarchies in fact seem to offer the only means of defending the fundamental rights of the poor, there is always the danger of over-estimating their role to the detriment of the efforts of the laity and popular or political organisations which should normally carry this burden. To be the 'voice of those who have no voice' can give the clergy some prestige at any given moment, but as a permanent situation it can prevent the poor from being the agents of their own liberation and of the struggle for their own rights.
There is always the temptation to over-personalise the rights of the poor. The poor not only need personal rights but also need the collective rights of their own organisations. This does not happen with other social classes where individuals have wider options. Many clergymen have understood this and have widened the scope of the Church's struggle to include the collective rights of workers and peasants.

To guarantee the rights of the weak is to guarantee the rights of all the people of Latin America; to guarantee the rights of the privileged classes is to violate the rights of all the rest.

Translated by John Macdonald

Notes

1. Fr. Joseph Marins and his team have published an impressive compendium of facts and documented evidence about these Christians: *Praxis del Martirio ayer y hoy* (Bogotá 1977).

2. This article was written during the first half of 1978, other important statements and facts may have emerged since then.

Norbert Greinacher

The Responsibility of the Churches in the First World for Establishing Human Rights

IN THIS issue so far, articles—particularly those by W. Huber and J. M. Lochman—have shown the ambiguity of basing human rights wholly on individual liberty; and they have called attention to the struggle to extend them to include social rights. Up till now the whole problem of establishing human rights for all men has suffered from this antithesis. This is most plainly seen in the west's current policy concerning human rights.

Since 1945 the churches in the First World have gradually realised the significance of individual human rights and their Christian implications; sometimes they even became staunch champions of these rights. By so doing they often added a religious dimension to their recognition. A leading factor in this process has been the legitimate and reasonable interest of the churches in calling special attention to the need to achieve religious and academic liberty, within the general framework of individual human rights. However, as a result, whether they realise it or not, the First World churches are falling into the grave danger of giving a religious veneer of legality to the existing national and international capitalist economic structures, and to all the injustices that go with them. Frequently the Catholic Church in the First World has overlooked the fact that the statements by Pope John XXIII, Pope Paul VI and the documents of the Second Vatican Council are far more progressive in this field than are her own. Characteristically, for example, the Federal Republic of Germany has received the propositions of Pope Paul VI's

Encyclical *Populorum Progressio* (26th March 1967) with minimal interest.

1. THE PRESENT WORLD ECONOMIC ORDER AND HUMAN RIGHTS

The first World Development Report of the World Bank (15th August 1978) has shown up afresh the shocking injustice that lies hidden beneath the present 'order' of the world economy. There is a world population of some four thousand million people. Of that number there are, at the time of writing, around eight hundred million men and women living deprived and painful lives; they suffer from malnutrition, lack of public health care, a high infant mortality-rate, low life-expectation and a degrading environment. And in the year A.D. 2000 there is every likelihood that six hundred million people will still be living in absolute poverty.

The worst aspect of this horrific disaster is that the First World barely registers it. Yet it is indisputable that by strenuous effort it could have been averted. The First World is content to give Development Aid amounting to 0·36 per cent of the GNP: in real terms little more than the publicity costs on export profits in world trade.[2] The First and, increasingly, the Second World live at the expense of the Third and Forth World. As they enjoy a standard of living that is always rising, they fail to admit to themselves who is paying the bill.

In the last analysis today's world economic order represents a projection of clas ical eighteenth and nineteenth century bourgeois individualism and egoism in regard to property and possessions onto a world scale. Only now it is a question of the relative position of the affluent and the poor nations in the world as a whole. Even today the affluent nations stress their right to property—in other words, to their standard of living. They insist that this right of theirs should be recognised by the very nations who are living below the subsistence level. It is in this way that the current world economic order—and its ideological defence—can be called an explicit expression of the bourgeois ideology already described. No one ought to be surprised that it is precisely this world economic order which is experienced in the Third and Fourth World as exploitation. In the present circumstances the insistence by the First and Second World nations, on their so-called 'property' is downright mockery in the ears of the poor nations. It must surely be patently clear, even to a very enlightened liberal, to an advocate of a social market economy, that free enterprise can only work between partners of equal strength. In the Encyclical *Populorum Progressio* Pope Paul VI rightly declares:

> The consent of the parties does not suffice to guarantee the justice of their contract . . . an economy of exchange can no longer be based solely on the law of free and unbridled competition, a law which, in its turn,

too often creates an economic dictatorship. Freedom of trade is right and fair only if it is subject to the demands of social justice (Item 59).

The Easter Declaration 1978 of the French Papal Commission *Justitia et Pax* summarises the conclusions as follows: 'The political order is sick . . . when the developed countries spend more than 500 billion dollars on their defence while their official Development Aid in the same year (1974) amounts to just 12 billion dollars. The economic order is sick . . . when 10 per cent of the world's population suffers gross malnutrition and 50 per cent (i.e., 2 000 000 000 people) suffer dietary deficiencies or lack of food. . . . This order, which is sick in so many ways, is the result of the craving for domination—in short, what we call "sin". We are not able to see the other man if we are attempting to be his master. And we cannot see God if we use him—in any way at all—to justify and achieve domination.'[3]

The problems outlined here grow even more acute with the so-called new world economic order.[4] The call for a change in the existing international systems of trade and currency was already sounding loud and clear in 1964 when the first World Trade Conference (U.N.C.T.A.D. I) was convened in Geneva. It was then that the historic alliance of developing countries was forged: the 'Group of 77'. Since that time the membership has risen to a total of some 120 countries. A comprehensive list was drawn up of demands from developing countries, calling for the creation of a new world economic order. This was debated in particular at the sixth Special Session of the General Assembly of the United Nations in the spring of 1974. It was at this session too that the Declaration and Programme of Action on the Establishment of a New International Economic Order was passed. This Declaration is perfectly correct when it says: 'It has proved to be impossible to achieve an equitable development of the communities of nations within the framework of the existing world economic order'.[5]

These resolutions meant that the new world economic order must be based on the following principles: Recognition of and respect for the sovereign equality of all nations; the right of every country to determine for itself its economic and social system, to control its own resources and, if necessary, to nationalise them; the right of liberation from any colonial or racial regime, of compensation for any exploitation of resources during the period; the right of support for independence-movements; the creation of reasonable and proper ratios between prices for exports and imports for the under-developed countries; the reform of the international monetary system; the supervision of the activities of multinational companies, and a growth of exchange in technology.

The more cordially we welcome the principles of this Declaration, the more squarely we must also face the question: Are the demands of the Programme of Action able, in fact, to lead to a decisive improvement of the situation, and to a juster order? There are weighty arguments to support the contention that the new world economic order represents merely a reform of the old conditions and relationships of dependence—certainly not their abolition. Consider for a moment Johan Galtung's hypothesis. He suggests that there are not only political and economic forms of dependence between the (rich) 'central' nations and the (poor) 'marginal' ones, but also that there are to some extent special associations and a coincidence of interests between the political and industrial elite in the central nations and 'bridge-head personnel' (i.e., elite) in the marginal nations.[6] Now if this is right, the grave danger exists that this new world economic order will benefit primarily the multi-national concerns and the bridge-head elite working with them in the developing countries. This possibility was also clearly recognised by the Catholic and Protestant churches in West Germany. The occasion was the Conference U.N.C.T.A.D. IV, and they were able to clarify their common attitudes in their statement: 'We must be aware of the danger that even a new international order which abolishes the disadvantages of the old system can turn into an instrument of domination—using either existing or new levers of industrial, technological or military power. For this reason this new order must . . . include a genuine re-distribution of resources, technologies and powers of decision-making'.[7] So several things are clear. Most of the industrial nations, notably USA and West Germany, are strongly opposed to meeting the claims made by the under-developed nations. The new world economic order is ambivalent, to say the least, and under no circumstances will it lead to a qualitatively new structure of the economy that would particularly benefit the exploited classes in the under-developed countries. This new world economic order will suffer, like its predecessor, from the fundamental *malaise* of the rich nations, namely 'collective individualism of ownership' if the phrase may be forgiven. The order also shows the mark, I think, of an ill-balanced interpretation of individual human rights. When we consider that this world economic order often gains further acceptability by human rights' being understood individualistically, we can see that it would bring into disrepute the commitment to individual human rights that is so absolutely essential for the days ahead as well.

2. NECESSARY STEPS TO COMPLEMENT THE INDIVIDUAL ASPECT OF HUMAN RIGHTS

The United Nations took an important step on this road to amending the classically individual design of human rights in the Human Rights Convention of 16th December 1966. As Part One of its document, it issued an *International Covenant on Economic, Social and Cultural Rights.* In the preamble, the United Nations quite rightly proceeded from the premiss 'that, in accordance with the Universal Declaration of Human Rights, the ideal of free human beings enjoying freedom from fear and want can only be achieved if conditions are created whereby everyone may use his economic, social and cultural rights, as well as his civil and political rights'. In the itemised Articles that ensue the following rights are then specified: The right of peoples to self-determination; freedom in decision-making over their political status and their economic, social and cultural development; free power of disposal of their natural and industrial resources; the right to work; the right to just, safe and healthy conditions of work, fair wages, sufficient means of livelihood; the right to recreation, leisure and holidays; the right to form Trade Unions; the right to strike; the right to social security; maximum protection of the family; the right to a reasonable standard of living, adequate nutrition, clothing and housing and the right to a steady improvement of living conditions; protection from hunger; a just distribution of the world's store of foodstuffs; the highest standard of physical and mental health; the right to education and participation in cultural life; freedom of science and art; the right of peoples to enjoy and have full and free use of their natural and industrial resources.

It could clearly be a problem to relate the rights of the individual listed above and the mutual rights of nations to one another. Similarly the establishing of these rights will be immensely complex. But we must realise with equal clarity just how drastically and necessarily human rights have been extended in comparison with their traditional western formulations. But notice that it was not the Christian churches who had identified themselves with this long over-due task of extended amendment; it was the 'children of this world'. In this fight, as in the struggle for individual human rights, they were basically more Christian than the churches. For it is beyond dispute that right from the New Testament onwards, however individual human rights might appear to be, they had to be given a social meaning. It has been especially important that the areas of industrial relationships, political power-structures and education should not be regarded as though they were some kind of foreign territories where human rights have no meaning. No, these too should be areas of application of human rights. We are then in a positon to see the intimate connection between relationships of dependence of an essentially economic and political character and the denial of human rights. The world's economic market has been exploited without restraint by the rich nations and the multi-national concerns; they have misused it with an eye solely to their own advantage; there is no question at all of a free market between partners with equal rights. This is the basic reason why

800 million people cannot live above subsistence level. This is also how the right to life itself is denied to millions of people through this false understanding of the right of ownership, whether private or collective. It is only when all these facts have been clearly recognised that it will be possible for a genuinely new and just world economic order to emerge. The truth is that the First World has to realise that in the final analysis and in the long-term it is in its own deepest interests to solve these planetary social conflicts. It is the prevention of social war between north and south that offers the only chance of survival for the First World itself.

3. WHAT ACTION CAN THE CHURCHES IN THE FIRST WORLD TAKE?

If we do proceed from the position that for hundreds of millions of human beings the satisfying of their basic needs is made impossible by the world economic order as it actually exists, and that it stands for a permanent denial of their individual and social human rights, then this throws down an enormous challenge to the Christian churches—particularly the First World churches. Admittedly it is essential to appreciate that the chances of the churches' influencing the world economic order are extraordinarily slim. But this must not be an excuse for doing nothing. Some tasks of the churches in the First World should be presented as a challenge.

1. It is highly necessary for the First World churches to create among their members, and especially among their office-bearers, an awareness of what is at stake. It has to be recognised, of course, that after the war many national churches did provide a wide range of assistance to the Third and Fourth Worlds, both in money and manpower. However the main concept behind this, whether it was consciously held or not, was the idea of a caring or agapeic help: the rich man helps the poor man. In no way should such charitable help be denigrated. It is, as always, necessary and meaningful. The same applies to help given by individual church communities for another church, by way of sponsoring. But the deepest necessity of all is for church members to start to appreciate that this is a matter of structures of dependence, politico-economic in character, and that in addition to the charitable help, political measurers are absolutely imperative. But first the conviction has to grow that in our situation today obedience to the commandment of Christian love of our neighbour requires above all a political commitment to alter the politico-economic structures. Pope Paul VI's Encyclical, *Populorum Progressio,* took this into account but it was precisely in this respect that the First World practically ignored it. It must also be a prime and urgent duty of the churches' relief organisations themselves to point out these structural connections in their publicity work.

2. In the industrial companies of the First World the poor nations of

the Third and Fourth World have virtually no lobby. It is fitting for the Christian churches, as disciples of Jesus Christ, to speak up for the poor nations, making their voice heard, come wind come weather, for those who have no voice. They will thus rouse the guilty conscience in our society. In West Germany the 'Workfellowship of Catholic communities of undergraduates and other students' have attempted this in their excellent statement on 'The Church in Latin America'. They say there among other things; 'From now on we must intensify our efforts to make public opinion really aware of this fact: there exists a connection of cause and effect between the life-situation of the majority of Latin America's population (characterised as it is by wretchedness, oppression and exploitation) and the power-structures of the world economic order that prevails. It is only the rich who ultimately gain from this connection: they become richer still'.[8] The Churches must start making a greater effort than hitherto to create an awareness of an unwelcome problem: the nations in the First World cannot dodge the fact that they must cut down their material necessities. It is important to give development aid; it is even more important to appreciate that the First World nations are getting what does not belong to them, and on a much greater scale as development-aid is put into effect. The Memorandum of the Catholic and Protestant Churches in West Germany strikes the right note: 'If a new and fairer world economic order is to emerge, bringing the need to take far-reaching decisions in the realm of politics, drastic structural changes will have to be affected in our economy and society. If the object of a new order is to enable all men to have a just share of the essential resources of this earth (and that would mean, as a start, helping millions of people to satisfy their basic needs), then the very first question to be put must be: "Doesn't this make it necessary for individuals to radically change their way of life in every-day matters affecting work, spending and leisure?" '[9]

What must not happen is that these necessary reductions take effect at the expense of the socially weak in the industrial companies of the First World. It will not be enough just to cut down the income of the upper classes. On the contrary, there is also need for reductions in wide sections of the middle class. It must be perfectly possible for the wealthy nations to change the present utterly unjust situation by the self-denial that reason dictates and that has traditionally been expressed by commending the willingness to sacrifice. It is the Churches which are the institutions that could make sense of the concept of self-denial. Although the Churches have often abused this idea in order to establish their own authority, they have also been known to use it before to promote brotherliness. This is the way that the Churches can use it in their epoch-making task, and, to say the least, they are in practice the only organised representatives of the concept of denying one's possessions for the sake of brotherliness.

3. If the Churches of the First World do provide help for the Third and Fourth World, the most important consideration will be to provide support for those people who are exerting pressure for the total liberation of the oppressed and exploited. Admittedly it is difficult to discover the appropriate criteria; it is specially hard to decide in a particular case as to whether help that is being offered in good faith will in the end result in liberating people or in strengthening the *status quo*. In this connection in West Germany the Bishops' statement *Adveniat* has led to a public discussion of its theme.[10] It is also common knowledge that a passionate debate is being waged over the financial grants of the World Council of Churches to political movements that use violence. These problems cannot be taken further here. But what is absolutely basic is that the churches must discourage everything that could intensify the state of oppression in the Third and Fourth World; even if it is only a matter of the ideological recognition of political systems. Instead the Churches must encourage everything that leads to the liberation of these nations. Here too the Church can bring her whole influence to bear so that political asylum is granted less grudgingly to persecuted political refugees from the developing countries.

4. The Christian Church—and the Catholic Church in particular—is one of the few moral institutions on a world scale that there really are. Experience shows that on those occasions when problems of the world community are set out judiciously and clearly and their ethical implications credibly represented, world opinion is not heedless. (See, for example, the reports concerning the 'Club of Rome', and the response to them). The Churches must not forbear from exposing the blatant injustice of the existing world economic order. At the same time it should continue to appeal to men's consciences to commit themselves to the full establishment of human rights.

Translated by T. C. Baird

Notes

1. At the time of writing this article, there were unfortunately only press reports available. See for example the *Süddeutsche Zeitung* of 17th August 1978.

2. Thus sometime in the year 1976 2·3 billion came back in orders for the German economy from 3·48 billion DM nett contributions of West Germany's government development aid.

3. Cited from *Publik-Forum* of 11th August 1978.

4. See D. Krebschull and others in *Die Neue Wetwirtschaftsordnung* (Hamburg 1977); R. Jonas-M. Tietzel *Die Neuordnung der Weltwirtschaft* (Bonn 1976).

5. D. Krebschull, *ibid.* p. 46.

6. See especially J. Galtung *Eine Strukturelle Theorie des Imperialismus* in: D. Senghaas (ed.) *Imperialismus und Strukturelle Gewalt. Analysen über abhängige Reproducktion* (Frankfurt 1972) pp. 29-104; J. Galtung *Strukturelle Gewalt. Beiträge zur Friedens- und Konfliktforschung* (Hamburg 1975).

7. H. Kunst—H. Tenhumberg *Sozial Gerechtigkeit und internationale Weltwirtschaftsordnung* (Munich 1976) pp. 9 ff.

8. 'Kirche in Lateinamerika. Stellungsnahme der Delegierten-versammlung der "Arbeitsgemeinschaft katholischer Studenten- und Hochschul-gemeinden"' of 1st August 1978 *Publik-Forum* of 25th August 1978.

9. H. Kunst—H. Tenhumberg, *loc. cit.* p. 25.

10. See 'Dokumentation zum Memorandum wetsdeutscher Theologen zur Kampagne gegen die Theologie der Befreiung' (mimeographed ms), and also the declaration mentioned in footnote 8.

Denis E. Hurley

What can the Church Do to Overcome Apartheid?

THERE ARE three ways of overcoming apartheid: by violent revolution, by economic war or by peaceful evolution.

Some would maintain that the conditions for a just revolutionary war obtain in South Africa. Possibly they do, except in regard to the outcome. At this moment in history the outcome, short of armed intervention by a world power, is likely to be total devastation. Anyhow, it is unrealistic to talk of the Church getting involved in war.

All out economic war is becoming a popular choice. Some Black leaders in South Africa say that they are willing to face the immediate consequences in view of the ultimate result. Other people maintain that all out economic war can be envisaged only as one aspect of a more general struggle involving military dimensions as well: 'Those who seek to bring about change in South Africa's racial attitudes and policies by cutting us off from the capital markets of the world should understand clearly that in practice, if not intent, they are aiming at change by violence.'[1] It is practically impossible for the Church in South Africa to get involved in economic war. Advocating it on an occasional basis would not achieve much and since it would lead to imprisonment could easily be prevented from growing into a campaign—whether or not a campaign for such a cause in South Africa would ever catch on among people who must suffer the consequences. Churches outside South Africa might consider themselves justified in advocating economic war against South Africa but they should weigh all the implications.

We come now to peaceful evolution and ask ourselves what the Church can do about that. One experiences an almost overpowering desire to reply: 'Precious little', and leave it at that. If we give an ecumenical meaning to the word 'Church' and use the term to designate the whole complex of religious bodies in South Africa calling themselves Christian, ideally the Church, by courageous witness to its law of love, could dissolve apartheid tomorrow. But this will not happen because the strongest group of Churches among the whites, the Dutch Reformed Churches, accepts apartheid as a practical necessity in a sinful divided world; and the other Churches, the so-called English-speaking Churches[2] though officially and by decision of their leadership opposed to apartheid are light years away from the kind of practical corporate witness necessary to make a significant impact upon it.

Their leadership structures do indeed issue pronouncements. The Churches hold integrated meetings of synods, councils and committees. They provide for men of all races to hold high office. Some of these Churches foster, to a certain extent, the integration of institutions like seminaries, convents and schools. They also foster integrated groups and associations of laity and events like retreats, training courses and seminars.

There are places where people of different race worship together regularly in the same church but this is not as common a feature as it should be. There are two major obstacles: the geographical separation of residential areas and linguistic and cultural differences. And even when people of different race worship together and receive communion at the same table there is little, if any, Christian community outside the church.

From this it can be gathered that despite what may appear to be commendable efforts on the part of certain elements in the Church the bulk of the membership remains almost totally unaffected.

This brings us to the principal hindrance to progress in the churches officially committed to overcoming apartheid: social attitudes. If we knew how to influence the social attitudes of the great body of Christians we would know what the Church could do to overcome apartheid. In its impotence to do very much perhaps the Church of South Africa is proclaiming to the Church Universal that here is an issue that needs urgent attention.

It would appear that social attitudes are responsible for most of the evil rampant in the world—stupendous and calamitous evil yet, on analysis, not easily imputable to individuals or, if so, to very few.

Thinking of all the evil done by colonialism, capitalism, nazism, fascism, marxism, racialism, nationalism, tribalism and every other social or political system we may well ask ourselves how many of the practitioners, at least among the rank and file, and that means the vast majority, have really sinned in the true moral sense. Nearly always, they have been motivated by social attitudes—blinding, stunting social attitudes. This is not a denial of personal guilt. But when we look at a vast accumulation of social evil we cannot but be struck by the disproportion between the cause, in terms of genuine personal choice and decision, and the catastrophic dimensions of the effect, in terms of social evil. If we take, for example, the outbreak of war in 1914 there is just no proportion between the decision to go to war and the consequences of the decision. And how many of those who made the decision had any moral qualms about it? Their inherited attitudes to politics and war were little influenced by moral conscience.

Once a man is socialised into the habits of a group, these habits constitute a sort of nervous system regulating his behaviour. His freedom of choice is severely restricted by the limits of his awareness and his awareness is profoundly conditioned by social habits. You can grow to maturity and beyond it in a society surviving and thriving on injustice, as white South African society does, and never aware of it. You can be part of a great system of evil and never know it. All because of social attitudes.

Social attitudes produce institutions and institutions in turn perpetuate attitudes. In this vicious circle evil institutions are both the effect and the cause of evil attitudes and, as Laurenti Magesa puts it, 'The worst type of sin, in fact the only "mortal sin" which has enslaved man for the greater part of his history, is the institutionalised sin. Under the institution vice appears to be, or is actually turned into, virtue. Aparthy towards evil is thus engendered; recognition of sin becomes totally effaced; sinful institutions become absolutised, almost idolised, and sin becomes absolutely mortal. The prerequisite of repentance in the Holy Scriptures (as, happily, in the Catechism) is recognition and admission of sinfulness. But recognition of evil, and therefore repentance for sin, is made practically impossible when sin is idolised as an institution.'[3]

Institutionalised evil is socialised evil, evil woven of the tough threads of social attitudes. Apartheid is such an evil. From the point of view of the Church, what we need in our effort to cope with it is a pastoral theology of social change.

Liberation theology is making its contribution to this kind of pastoral theology. It owes its origin in large measure to the genius of Joseph Cardijn who saw that the weakness of the Church in dealing with social evil stemmed from its abstract theology and 'teacher tell' pedagogy. Cardijn was not a theologian by profession but the system he elaborated for the training of young workers, emphasising life, gospel, community, discovery and action has helped to revolutionise theology, particularly in its pastoral aspects.

Is it posible to elaborate a pastoral praxis that would enable Christians to deal with a political establishment that is responsible for injustice and remains blind and stubborn in maintaining its position? Nothing can be more granite-like than social attitudes that are the fossilisation of power and wealth. Is revolution the only way to crack the granite? Or is it possible to work out a Christian method of dissolving the social attitudes of dominant groups? Paulo Freire answers in the negative. 'It is only the oppressed who by freeing themselves can free their oppressors. The latter, as an oppressor class, can free neither others nor themselves.'[4]

On the face of it, the methods that owe their origin to the 'see, judge, act' of Cardijn should be equally as effective in dealing with oppressors as with the oppressed. However, in the case of oppressors there is an additional problem, the problem of motivation. In the case of the oppressed, there is a certain attraction in a method that promises you an active role in your own liberation. But if you belong to the oppressing group you withdraw instinctively from involvement that brings you face to face with your own situation of guilt, previously possibly unsuspected, and drags you, if you persevere through the anguish of conversion.

All this may sound rather strange to people who have no experience of belonging to an oppressive society, but in fact we need a pastoral theology for oppressors as much as we do for the oppressed. In cases where the pursuit of justice means a radical change in the situation of an oppressing society, as it would for instance in regard to white society in South Africa, any member of that society who wishes to identify himself with the pursuit of justice must first undergo a radical change, a deep personal conversion. For some it can be agonising. It can demand the heroic.

Since South Africa is an almost exact image, in miniature, of the world situation of haves and have-nots, in that 17 per cent of the population, that is, the whites, control 70 per cent of the country's resources, there is possibly much to learn from the South African experience that is of importance for the world at large.

South Africa's present crisis arises from the failure of religious and cultural agencies to bring about change in the social attitudes of its dominant white minority. The crisis into which the world is moving seems also to stem from the failure of religious and cultural agencies to effect a sufficiently rapid transformation in the attitude of the societies that dominate the global economy to the detriment of less developed societies.

No single agency can hope to tackle this problem alone with even minimal hope of success. It is a problem that permeates the whole body of human society and every aspect of it. It is a social, cultural, political and economic problem—but fundamentally a moral problem and therefore a religious one. The Church must play its part, not in isolation from but in very close collaboration with other social institutions and agencies.

In what should the role of the Church consist? Formulating the answer as succinctly as possible I would say: in developing and promoting a pastoral theology of social change.

Ecclesial revolutions take longer than political ones. The theological revolution that began haltingly enough in the early days of the nineteenth century is coming into full bloom a century and a half later. The Pilgrim Church has trod a rough road from the days of Möhler and the tragic La Mennais through Newman, Ketteler and *Rerum Novarum* and the great reforming movements in biblical studies, theology, liturgy, catechesis, lay involvement and social concern that reached an extraordinary and unified climax in Vatican II.

The theological revolution has been substantially accomplished. Now, we need to communicate it, to make it the daily fare of the Church universal. For this we need a pastoral theology of social change.

We have all the ingredients of a new Christian humanism, a view of the world and of life drawing vision and power from the Christ of the gospels and the resurrection, alive, present and active in the Church and seeking through us to bring a Christian consecration to man's co-operation with God in the unfolding of the mystery of creation.

The new Christian synthesis far outshines anything that marxism or any purely human democracy has to offer. But we have got to be able to communicate it. This is our weak point at the moment: communication. It is the heritage of a long period of abstract theology, far removed from life experience, and of pedagogical methods scarcely calculated to arouse, to enthuse and to convert.

When I speak of communication I speak not only of intellectual communication but of that totality of approach in communication that leads to conviction and conversion, to a new praxis. Already much has been learned in the Church in this regard and much is practised, but in a spasmodic, unsystematic and fragmented way. What we need is a pastoral theology of social change that will affect the Church as a whole, in all its leaders, teachers and communicators, a pastoral theology that will transform our faculties and seminaries and our religious and pastoral institutes and make them capable of turning out the apostles of the new Pentecost.

The new pastoral theology must use the tools of the human sciences to discover how social attitudes develop and operate and how they can be changed, and must be willing to advocate training in the most modern methods of experiential learning. Social attitudes are among the toughest fibres of our being. We shall need an alliance of the full force of the gospel and of scientific method to learn how to deal with them.

The first reaction of many people, including scientifically trained people, to this kind of talk is: 'Forget it, you can do nothing about social attitudes. Change the situation, change the structures, and the attitudes will change of themselves.' There is a lot of truth in this. In the South African context it simply means that the only way is violent revolution. And realistically, that is how it looks at present.

However, taking the South African experience as a starting point, a Christian reflection based on the power of the risen Christ and his Spirit must come to grips with the issue of social attitudes, realise the part they play in the matter of social evil and endeavour to work out a practical pastoral approach.

The aim of the Church is to work with Christ in the transformation of mankind. Such transformation, like everything that involves man, has two dimensions: the personal and the social. In the life of the Church up to the present we have paid a good deal of attention to the personal, now it is time to concentrate equal attention, and possibly even more, on social transformation.

Such a development in pastoral theology could have a profound effect on all our methods of evangelisation, on catechesis, liturgy, preaching, pastoral ministry and lay apostolate. We would be coming close to the bone in what are the most powerful forces motivating human behaviour—social attitudes. When these are distorted, as some inevitably are in every human society, they are the most vivid illustration of original sin and the most insidious temptation to Manicheism.

Notes

1. H. Oppenheimer *Why the World Should Continue to Invest in South Africa:* Address to the International Monetary Conference, Mexico City, 22nd May 1978 (Johannesburg).

2. The major English-speaking churches in South Africa are the Methodist, Anglican, Roman Catholic and Lutheran churches. Though the majority of adherents speak an African language, English is usually the common language of synods and other assemblies and of communication on a national level.

3. Laurenti Magesa 'The Biblical Foundation for a Liberation Theology for Africa', *Africa Service Bulletin* No. 39 (April 1977 Lusaka, Zambia).

4. P. Freire *Pedagogy of the Oppressed.* (New York) Chapter 1, page 42.

Contributors

JOSEF BLANK was born in 1926 and Ludwigshafen and ordained as priest 1951. Since 1969 he has been Professor of NT Exegesis and Biblical Theology at the University of the Saarland in Saarbrücken. His publications include *Krisis* (1964), *Paulus und Jesus* (1968), *Weiss Jesus mehr vom Menschen?* (1971), *Der Mensch am Ende der Moral* (1971), *Jesus von Nazareth. Geschichte und Relevanz* (1972).

JAMES A. CORIDEN, STL, JCD, JD, is Dean of the Washington Theological Union. He was born in 1932 and is a priest of the Diocese of Gary, Indiana (USA). He is an active member of the Canon Law Society of America and has edited several volumes of its sponsored studies; the most recent is *Sexism and Church Law: Equal Opportunity and Affirmative Action* (New York 1977). He has contributed several articles on canonical topics to journals including *Concilium, Jurist, Chicago Studies, Journal of Ecumenical Studies*, and *Studia Canonica.*

SEGUNDO GALILEA is of Chilean nationality. He was born in Santiago in 1922 and was ordained in 1956. Since 1963 he has worked closely with CELAM and CLAR (Conference of Religious in Latin America), organising pastoral and spiritual workshops throughout the continent. He has published many articles and books such as the following: *Evangelización en América Latina* (1969), *Espiritualidad de la liberación* (1973).

MARIA GORETTI and DOMINGO SALE. For security reasons, the two authors, known to the editors, publish that article under pseudonyms.

NORBERT GREINACHER was born in 1931 at Freiburg im Bresgau (Germany). He was ordained priest in 1956. He is Professor of Practical Theology at the University of Tübingen. The following are some of his publications: *Soziologie der Pfarrei* (Freiburg 1955), *Die Kirche in der städtischen Gesellschaft* (Mainz 1966), *Bilanz des deutschen Katholizismus* (Mainz 1966), *In Sache Synode* (Düsselldorf 1970).

WOLFGANG HUBER was born in 1942. He is Deputy Director of the Research Institute of the Evangelische Studiengemeinschaft and Privatdozen in the Faculty of Theology at the University of Heidelberg. His publications include *Passa und Ostern* (1969), *Was heisst Friedensforschung?* (1971, with G. Picht) and *Menschenrechte—Perspektiven einer menschlichen Welt* (1977, with H. E. Todt).

DENIS E. HURLEY, OM, Archbishop of Durban, was born of Irish parents at Cape Town, South Africa in 1915, ordained priest in 1939, and consecrated bishop in 1947. He has served as president of the Southern African Catholic Bishops' Conference 1952-1960, and was appointed member of Central Preparatory Commission of Second Vatican Council, 1961. He attended the Vatican Council and served as member of Commission for Priestley Formation and Christian Education. He attended the Synod of Bishops 1967, 1974 and 1977. He was president of the South African Institute of Race Relations 1965-1966.

JAMES LIMBURG is Associate Professor of Old Testament, Luther-Northwestern Seminaries, St Paul, Minnesota. From 1962-1978 he was Professor of Religion at Augustana College, Sioux Falls, South Dakota. His publications include *From Slavery to Nationhood* (Philadelphia 1977), *The Prophets and the Powerless* (Atlanta 1977) and various articles and reviews.

JAN MILIČ LOCHMAN was born in 1922 at Nové Mesto (Czechoslovakia). He studied theology and philosophy at Prague, St Andrews and Basle. He has taught as Professor of Theology at Prague and New York, and since 1969 he has occupied the chair of Systematic Theology at the University of Basle. For many years Professor Lochman has been active in the ecumenical movement. He is a member of the Faith and Order Commission of the World Council of Churches, and chairman of the theological section of the World Alliance of Reformed Churches. His publications include *Herrschaft Christi in der säkularisierten Welt* (Zürich 1967); *The Church in a Marxist Society* (New York and London 1970); *Christus oder Prometheus* (Hamburg 1972); *Marx begegnen, Was Christen und Marxistein eint und trennt* (Gütersloh 1977).

LEOPOLDO JUAN NIILUS is an Argentine lawyer, born in 1930, Tallinn, Estonia. Formerly a practising lawyer, Buenos Aires, and a founding member of the Argentine Institute of Science and Administration, and Institute de sociología Económica, Buenos Aires. He has participated in numerous major ecumenical consultations and enterprises. He has published *On Penal Law* (Essays) and articles and essays in several ecumenical publications.

STEPHAN H. P. PFÜRTNER was born in 1922 in Dahzig. From 1939-1945 he was officially attached to the army ambulance service in Poland and Russia but released to study medicine in Breslau and Kiel in the interim. He also studied philosophy and psychology. From 1942-43 he was imprisoned in Hamburg and Lübeck for religious and political opposition to the Nazi regime, and was condemned by the 'people's court' in Berlin and forbidden to attend the university. In 1945 he resumed studies in philosophy and began to study theology in Walberberg (near Bonn), Fribourg (Switzerland) and Rome. Since 1977 he has been professor for Social Ethics at Philipps University, Marburg. He is married with two children. His publications include *Triebleben und sittlichen Vollendung* (1958), *Luther und Thomas im Gespräch* (1961), *Moral—Was gilt heute noch?* (1972), *Kirche und Sexualität* (1972), *Macht, Recht und Gewissen in Kirche und Gesellschaft* (1972), *Politik und Gewissen—Gewissen und Politik* (1976), and numerous contributions to periodicals, lexica and other compilations.

BERNARD PLONGERON was ordained priest in Paris in 1964. After teaching in the Universities of Strasbourg and Louvain he is now assistant professor at the Institut Catholique de Paris (Arts and Theology) and serves on the staff and the National Committee of the Centre National de la Recherche Scientifique. A specialist in the history of religious thought in the society of the Ancien Régime and of the contemporary period, he has published some 50 articles in France and elsewhere, and several books, including *La vie quotidienne du clergé française au XVIIIe* (Paris 1974).

FRANÇOIS REFOULÉ, OP, was born in Orleans, France, in 1922 and ordained in 1950. He has been a university chaplain in Sweden, literary editor of *Cerf* since 1964 and Catholic secretary for the ecumenical translation of the Bible. He has written numerous articles on Tertullian, Augustine, Evagrius Ponticus and Luther, and his books include *Marx et Saint Paul* (1972).

CHARLES WACKENHEIM was born in 1931. A graduate of the Ecole Pratique des Hautes Etudes, D.Ph. (Paris) and D.Th. (Strasbourg), since 1962 he has been teaching fundamental theology at the Faculty of Catholic Theology in Strasbourg (Université des Sciences Humaines). His main publications are *La faillite de la religion d'après Karl Marx* (Paris 1963), *Christianisme sans idéologie* (Paris 1974), *La théologie catholique* (Paris 1977).